BURCH AT THE HELM

STARPATH

www.starpathpublications.com

ISBN 978-0-914025-39-9

Published by
Starpath Publications
3050 NW 63rd Street, Seattle, WA 98107
Manufactured in the United States of America
www.starpathpublications.com

CONTENTS

Preface iv

GENERAL NAVIGATION

Unofficial, Official Definitions & Conventions in Navigation 2

Hazards of Misinformation 5

The Rules Are Your Friend 7

Timekeeping in Navigation & Weather 10

Logbook Procedures 13

Compass Checks with the Sun 17

Open Source Navigation 19

INLAND & COASTAL NAVIGATION

Wrinkles in Practical ECS 23

Read the Chart! 29

Progress to Weather 32

Sextant Piloting 36

Traffic in the Fog 44

OCEAN & CELESTIAL NAVIGATION

The Ocean-going Nav Station 52

Ocean Dead Reckoning 57

Know Your Limits! 61

The Books of Celestial Navigation 64

"K" is for Communicate 68

Lunars! 72

MARINE WEATHER

Barometer Tactics 77

ASCAT — Wind at Sea 81

Navigation in Hurricane Season 85

Predicting Fog 89

The Corner Effect 93

OCEAN & TIDAL CURRENTS

Estimating and Correcting for Current Set 97

More Current Sailing 101

Coastal Currents 105

Ocean Currents Are Not What They Used To Be 109

Index 115

PREFACE

The articles included here were originally published in Blue Water Sailing magazine over a period of several years. They cover diverse topics, but each is intended to enhance the safety and efficiency of navigation. Though published in a magazine devoted to sailing, these subjects and the information contained applies to all vessels, power, sail, and paddle.

They have been regrouped by topic, so the order presented here does not reflect the order of original publication. For the most part they deal with special issues, not often covered in detail in standard references. Some were motivated by issues of the day when published, but we have updated all as needed with new resources on the topics.

Questions, comments, or contact with the author can be made by email to helpdesk@starpath.com. Other books and products from Starpath can be seen at www.starpath.com

GENERAL
NAVIGATION

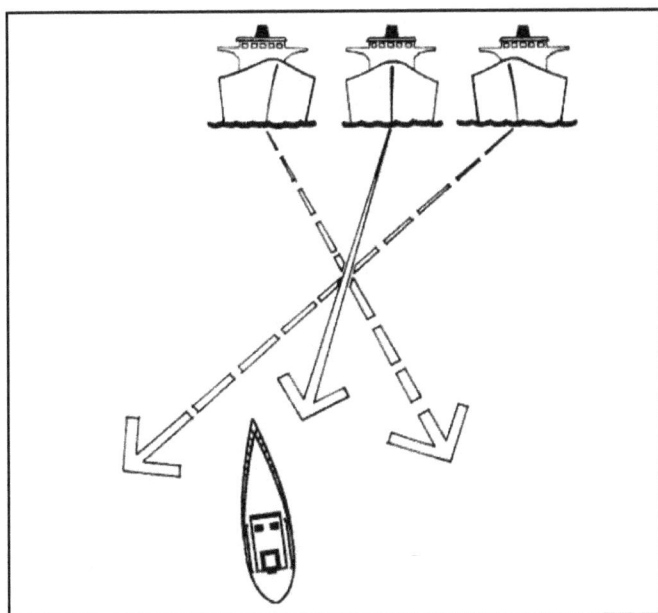

UNOFFICIAL, OFFICIAL DEFINITIONS & CONVENTIONS IN NAVIGATION

Like everywhere else on the boat, proper communication in navigation is always crucial to efficiency, and could be crucial to safety. Some conventions are widely used and long standing—to the point of being as much seamanship as navigation. Others, strangely enough, are evolving with time. They are different now than they were 10 years ago.

First the easy ones that comes up most often. All courses, headings, and bearings that are less than 100° should be preceded with leading zeros. Thus our course is 035 (oh, three, five), not 35 (three, five or thirty-five), and 005 (oh, oh, five) not 5. This is the way we should say them and write them. It should be considered not optional.

We deal with many angles in the nav station, especially when you get a sextant in your hand, so the goal here is to uniquely distinguish directions (headings, bearings, and courses) from everything else that might be an angle less than 100°.

Generally we should always specify the units of the directions, namely True, Magnetic, or Compass, but that rule can be demoted to an as-needed level, because we have so many rules that tell us what to use for specific subjects. For example, although the navigator cannot avoid using all three units (true, magnetic, and compass, no one else on the boat should have to deal with that. All courses and headings and bearings discussed on the boat and kept in the logbook should be Compass.

If someone wants to discuss true bearings or magnetic bearings that is fine, so long as they do not confuse the helmsman, which brings up a valuable tool that has wandered off of many modern ocean going yachts, namely, a *course box* or some equivalent. It is simply a way to post the correct course to steer in prominent view of the helm. Vessels from the Golden Age of Sailing all had one, and any ocean passage will point out their value—even if it is just piece of duct tape in clear view of the helm, with the latest course

printed boldly. Then cross it out and add a new one as it changes. It makes an easy way to keep track as watches change, or for a quick reference to check when the steering gets dicey.

The navigator can't avoid the other units because winds, currents, and swell directions are always given in True. Also, light sectors and range lines on nautical charts are always in True. A NE wind is one coming from 045 T. Swells are labeled like winds, the true direction they come from. A westerly swell is flowing from west to east. A current set of 135, on the other hand, means the water is flowing toward 135 T.

Angles *on the bow*, for navigation purposes or for wind directions, do not use leading zeros. We can say, for example, the apparent wind angle is 30° on the port bow. Bow angle winds are commonly used on sailboats: what is your wind angle? Answer: 30° apparent. The answer here assumes we know what tack we are on, but if you are recording this in the logbook, you must say 30° port or something like that. Another common use of bow angles is the piloting trick to find distance off. Measure the angle on the bow of a landmark, run a known distance, and then measure the bow angle again. From these data you can figure your distance off the landmark. These angles are likewise spoken and written without leading zeros.

On the other hand, larger vessels do not use port and starboard bow angles for recording apparent wind angles, but instead use proper relative bearings. Instead of 30° port, they would call this 330 R. On the starboard side, 30° starboard would now be 030 R. So even though both are relative to the bow, bow angles are considered angle increments, whereas relative bearings are considered directions. Relative bearings using this convention are common in radar work on vessels of any size. The EBL (electronic bearing line) would be read as 022 R, not 22 R.

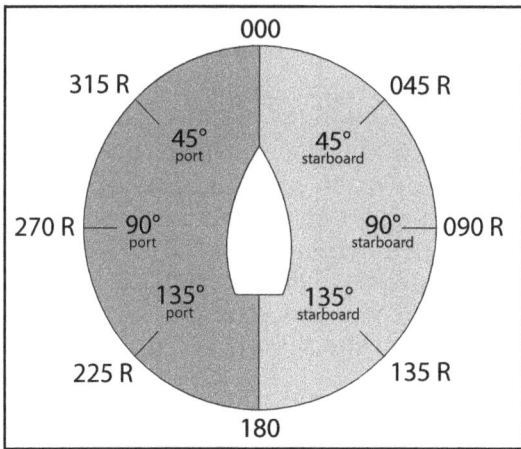

Figure 1. *Bow angles vs. relative bearings. Relative bearings are a direction relative to the bow and thus use leading zeros. Bow angles are thought of as a location on the bow, and thus do not use leading zeros.*

Another easy one. Times always include leading zeros. Thus the time is 0820, never 820. Likewise when recording or speaking times using seconds, we always use leading zeros: 03h 22m 06s.

When reporting a position, it is conventional to give the Latitude first and then the Longitude, but even more important, give the labels N,S or E,W at the end of the angles. Thus I am located at 47° 23.4′N, 122° 20.5′ W. Latitudes and longitudes are best written without leading zeros.

In celestial navigation we deal with the declination of a star. The declination of a star is the latitude over which it circles the earth once a day. All declinations are written with the label N,S in front of the angle. Thus the star Arcturus with declination N 19° 11′ passes just north of the southern tip of the big island of Hawaii at latitude 18° 55′ N. All of the various coordinates and angles used in cel nav do not use leading zeros, ie they are not directions, so they do not use leading zeros.

We can optimize our communications in the electronics world by distinguishing between course and speed over ground (COG, SOG) and course and speed made good (CMG, SMG). COG and SOG are electronic navigation terms made popular by Loran manufacturers when we first had convenient access to this valuable data, though the phrases were used long before then. There were competing terms to COG and SOG originally, but these two won out—or so it seemed for some time. Now the competition begins all again. The contestants include: electronics makers, NMEA, the IMO, navigation teaching facilities, and all the rest of us as end users.

It is more important than might appear, and with more interesting history and intrigue than we would ever guess. For now let me just seed the ground by proposing that COG be restricted to the instantaneous course I am now achieving relative to the fixed ground that I read and have knowledge of from my GPS. Likewise for the SOG; it is an output from the GPS that tells how

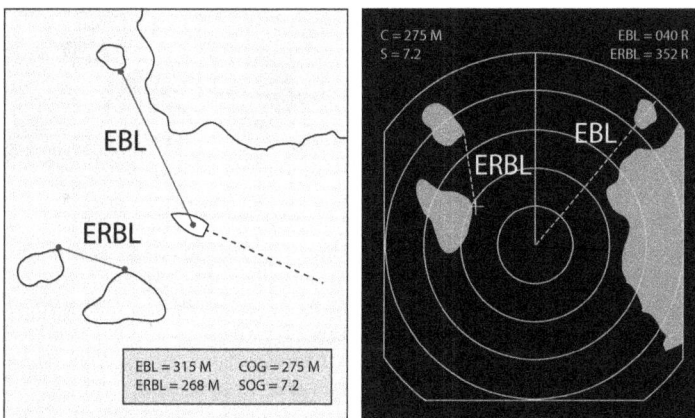

Figure 2. *A fine distinction in terminology that promotes good communications. An electronic bearing line (EBL) measures bearings from the boat; an electronic range and bearing line (ERBL) measures from an arbitrary point on the display. These are used on both echart displays and on radar screens. On electronic charts, the EBLs and ERBLs always include range as well. In radar the range from the vessel is measured with a VRM (variable range marker).*

fast I am moving at this moment relative to the ground.

CMG and SMG, on the other hand, are more flexible terms that are used to describe what we compute or anticipate our course and speed would be based on some correction to the knot-meter and compass. The terms are also used in a rather different context to describe the net progress achieved between two times, regardless of compass or knotmeter.

Thus if I steer 200 M at 6 kts with a current of 2 kts on my port beam, then I can solve a vector plot (or compute some other way) to conclude that my course made good will be 218 M and my speed made good will be 6.3 kts. Or in their other context, if I am now 1.0 miles NW of where I started 15 minutes ago, then my CMG was 315 T and my SMG was 4.0 kts, regardless of what route I took or how my speed might have varied along the way.

Keeping these concepts separate will help us distinguish what we are doing (COG and SOG) with what we might have planned. Or when going back over a logbook we can compare what we were actually doing at specific times (COG and SOG) with what we achieved in the end (CMG and SMG).

To further illustrate that we are still struggling with electronic terminology, we only have to look at the VMG (velocity made good) output from our electronic charting systems (ECS). At one point in time VMG was purely wind data—how fast I am progressing upwind or downwind. Now we must be careful. Depending on what brand ECS we have and what options, it could be that, or it could be VMG to the next waypoint, totally unrelated to the wind. Some units only offer one or the other, some offer both. Raytheon Marine calls them VMG-wind and VMG waypoint. Furuno uses VMG (for wind, in tune with tradition) and they use VMC (velocity made course) for the progress to the next waypoint. This VMC is what NMEA calls WCV, waypoint closing velocity, though I have not seen this term at the user interface side. It is what you want to optimize if you are racing, or trying to evaluate one heading vs. another for any navigation reason. VMG (wind) is for sailing performance, not for navigation. In Loran C days, WCV was often called SOA on the output side, for Speed of Advance, but that was simply wrong. It is no longer used.

Before leaving the electronic world, I should point out the difference between an electronic bearing line (EBL) and an electronic range and bearing line (ERBL, pronounced "urbel"). These terms apply to measurement tools on both radar and ECS displays, though the ECS producers are slow to pick up the ball on the terminology. There is no controversy as there is with COG. The IMO specifies the distinction: EBL is measured relative to the boat; ERBL is arbitrary point to point, anywhere on the screen. Some radars refer to ERBL as a "floating EBL," which makes sense, but distracts from the value of a consistent terminology. Hopefully we will see more urbel speak in the future. As it turns out, some ECS and some radar have just one type, while others have both. The latter could easily promote their enhanced options by adopting the preferred names.

The power of the Internet lets us research maritime terms in great detail, in multiple languages, though conventions and preferences are harder to discern. The terms and conventions we use in our online courses can be seen at www.starpath.com/glossary. §

Figure 3. *Course boxes were a traditional way to keep the present course posted for all to see in the cockpit or wheelhouse. Some equivalent remains an asset to navigation on all vessels. Periodically these become available online from decommissioned vessels or antique sellers.*

HAZARDS OF MISINFORMATION

Maritime lore is permeated with high esteem for what is called "local knowledge." It means a kind of information not found in standard references, only known to locals, or to folks who have sailed a particular route many times. It is often considered prize information, and indeed it can be—if there were not value to the concept on some level, it would have fallen from such popular use.

On the other hand, part of sound marine education is learning to make careful evaluation of all input that affects our decision making. We cannot take things for granted without some background, no matter how often they are repeated. Part of the reason to study navigation is to learn what the dependable sources are. *Chart No. 1* to explain the charts and the Coast Pilots to explain navigational concerns not shown on the charts are two basics. The US Coast Pilots and their counterparts for international waters include a wealth of information, often in fine detail, about most waterways around the world.

Beyond the references, we can also prepare ourselves with fundamental knowledge of oceanography and meteorology. Then if we are given some special suggestions or information on navigation we can vet it against on our own knowledge and resources. If the new information is consistent with what is known in standard references, then we have confidence in its use. If it is contrary to what we know, then we must be very careful. In many cases, what is considered local or special knowledge is actually well documented in the standard references, and it is only considered special knowledge by those who are not familiar with the standard references.

Local knowledge can often go astray when someone with experience in one type of vessel projects it onto the needs of another type of vessel. You can go aground on routes that are sworn to be good by those who simply do not know how much water you draw. Another example is the often recommended summertime passage of the West Coast of sailing out 100 miles, then transit the coast, then come back in, which more often than not just adds two days to your voyage as you much enhance your chances of much worse conditions—compared to running right along the coast, just outside the sea buoys.

A famous example related to equipment is the shark that ate the taffrail log, which was repeated so often it became gospel in the minds of many mariners. If you have ever used one, you will know they fray off if not maintained properly, which will look like it was bit off by a fish. This piece of misinformation about the shark has likely contributed to decline in use of these devices, which is a great pity. They are one of the most accurate means of ocean navigation, totally independent of all electrical power, and tremendously dependable—provided they are maintained.

The motivation of this note, however, is a much more tragic story about misinformation. When the Somali pirates murdered four sailors in February of 2011, a New York Times article on the event from Feb 22, 2011 included several quotes about the skipper and crew of the vessel. One of them stated

"...friends said he often turned off his G.P.S. instrument because pirates had learned to use them as homing devices."

We might analyze the nuances of this sentence—something the editors and authors of the article apparently did not do—but that is not the point. It is a clear statement, and it is totally wrong. To what extent this misinformation contributed to the tragedy cannot be known, but we must guard against this sort of thing at all times. It is another shark, eating another taffrail log, just far more serious.

GPS instruments are receivers; they are not transmitters. They do not broadcast anything. They do not communicate with the satellites, they just listen to them. No one can home in on an operating GPS unit on your boat. Turning off the GPS has no affect whatsoever on your being detected by any one, with any kind of equipment; it just makes your own navigation more difficult.

If we were to look for nuances, we might speculate that "G.P.S. instrument" was intended to mean an AIS (automatic identification system), which does indeed broadcast your position, because that is what it is designed to do. But if that were the intended meaning, it would be stretching the sensibility of the rest of the sentence. Nevertheless, the actual published sentence is inexcusably wrong, and its implications were not appreciated.

It is the job of the navigator to question things. If you see a light on the horizon that is not supposed to be there, your job is to not rest until you know what is going on with it. Recall that a third mate (sailing as AB) on the Exxon Valdez told the third mate in charge twice that a light was on the wrong side of the bow, but all records indicate he did not take her seriously. §

Figure 1. *MV* Costa Concordia *run aground off the west coast of Italy January, 2012, relying on the skippers local knowledge of the area.*

Figure 2. *The damaged MV* Cosco Busan *after striking the bridge tower fender. There was a professional pilot on board who is tested on local knowledge to get the license. He also tested positive for a lot of other things after the allision with the bridge.*

THE RULES ARE YOUR FRIEND

The Nav Rules are indeed our friends—they were created with the mission of protecting us from harm. The official name is International Regulations for the Preventing Collisions at Sea, abbreviated COLREGS. In the US, we see these most often in the USCG publication called The Navigation Rules, International – Inland, which we do not exaggerate when calling it the most important book in navigation.

We tend to think of collisions in dramatic images of ships colliding with extensive destruction, not to mention the image we all have of some tragic encounter between sailboat and ship, but the Rules are intended to prevent all collisions, regardless of the damage or injury done. In short, the Rules also serve as a guideline for good behavior at sea that can save us unnecessary anxiety and maybe even save us some money on a bright sunny day when no one is hurt at all.

The point at hand was brought to our attention recently by a local sailor who called to describe an encounter, wondering what their rights were in the circumstance. It is a simple tale with several messages.

There were two sailors aboard a 30-foot sailboat under power approaching a narrow channel known locally as Hole in the Wall on the Swinomish Slough. As they approached the entrance they came up on a 42-foot powerboat pulling a 14-foot runabout on a 60-foot line that was headed toward the entrance, but at a very slow speed.

The sailors decided to overtake the powerboat which they could easily do without slowing down. After they passed the powerboat they found they had to come back in front of the power-er boat to align for the narrow channel ahead, which they did, and then they slowed down for the approach.

At this point, the power boat decided to increase its speed and in turn over take the sailboat, which it did, but at this point they were all getting closer to the entrance so the power boat had to do precisely what the sail boat did and turn in front of it.

The sailors watched this taking place and both realized that the trailing runabout might not make it past their bow. As they watched this take place, sure enough, the prop of the raised outboard on the runabout carved a nice deep, foot-long gouge in the gelcoat of the bow.

The sailors presumed this was a clear cut case of their rights violated, because a vessel is supposed to stay clear when it passes; but it is not really quite that simple. Essentially every maritime collision involves the violation of at least one Rule by both vessels involved. This fact alone, by the way, is adequate cause for learning and obeying the Rules. If you do so, you are statistically very unlikely to be ever involved in a collision.

In the encounter described we have a series of lessons. First, of course, a sailboat under power is a power boat, so none of the Rules that refer to sailing vessels apply. The initial decision of the sailboat to overtake may not have been prudent. If it were known that it would have to immediately come back in front of the overtaken vessel after passing, then it definitely was an error. Rule 13 requires that you stay clear of a vessel being overtaken, and coming back in front of it and slowing down is not staying clear.

The same applies to the power boat over taking the sailboat. Both were wrong on some level, but the sailboat might argue that it was far enough ahead that its maneuver was reasonable. The powerboat maneuver, on the other hand, was by definition wrong because of the outcome.

But we are still not up to the gouge. Both sailors on the sailboat watched that event develop. They even discussed its possibility. But they did nothing about it. In short, they were observing the risk of collision develop and not responding. The proper response would be 5 or more short blasts on an air horn. This could well have saved them the trouble of this encounter. The power-

Figure 1. *A popular long narrow channel in the Pacific Northwest that provides frequent opportunity to rely upon the Navigation Rules*

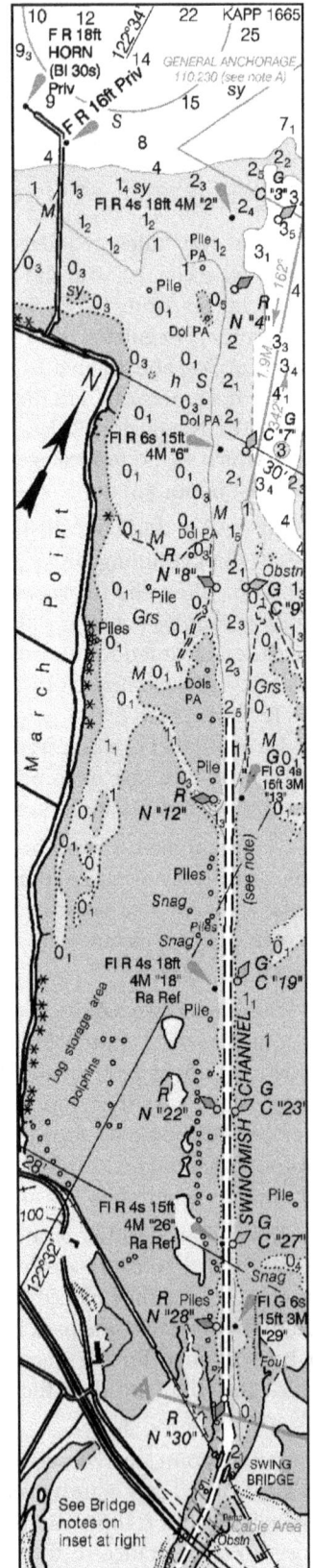

boat was not aware of what was taking place, nor that it even happened.

An air horn at hand for such events would be valuable. We should not sail into any questionable traffic situation without sounding the danger signal (Rule 34d). This rule applies to all vessels; sailboats can use it, just as ships and car ferrys use it.

Rule 34d. When vessels in sight of one another are approaching each other and from any cause either vessel fails to understand the intentions or actions of the other, or is in doubt whether sufficient action is being taken by the other to avoid collision, the vessel in doubt shall immediately indicate such doubt by giving at least five short and rapid blasts on the whistle. Such signal may be supplemented by a light signal of at least five short and rapid flashes.

Whenever we do use Rule 34d (called the danger or warning signal) we should also be considering stopping or slowing down. I do not know how fast things evolved in this incident, but that is always a factor in how we respond, which means we need to have our gear (air horns, flares, handheld VHF, handheld lights) in ready reach. It is easy to overlook these basics, whose need could come upon us with very short notice and in the most benign circumstances. The warning signal can also be given with flashes of a spot light, which could be more effective in some circumstances.

In any event, once you sound the danger signal—or certainly when you sound it the second time—you should be slowing down. Think of yourself explaining to the judge that you sounded the danger signal because you thought the situation was dangerous and did not know what was going to happen…. but you kept driving on in to it at the same course and speed.

Study of the Rules is a rewarding pastime, practical and captivating. They constitute a remarkable document with an immense assigned task—the prevention of collisions between a vast array of vessels in a vast array of circumstances: vessels barely visible at 100 yards to vessels the size of horizontal skyscrapers; drifting without power or traveling at 30 knots or more; following unmarked lanes or crisscrossing open waters offering nothing more than an educated guess as to their intended course; in all conditions of weather, clear or fog, calm or storm; and often with no common language between their drivers.

The USCG Navigation Rules book is 224 pages, but the part that covers steering and sailing rules (right of way) is just the 16 rules of Part B—a total of 12 pages. The rest covers important issues of lights, sounds, and general issues. All parts are important and in some ways interrelated, but mastering these 12 pages adds a lot of confidence to your navigation. At www.starpath.com/nav-pubs we made a pdf of these 12 pages that you can download and

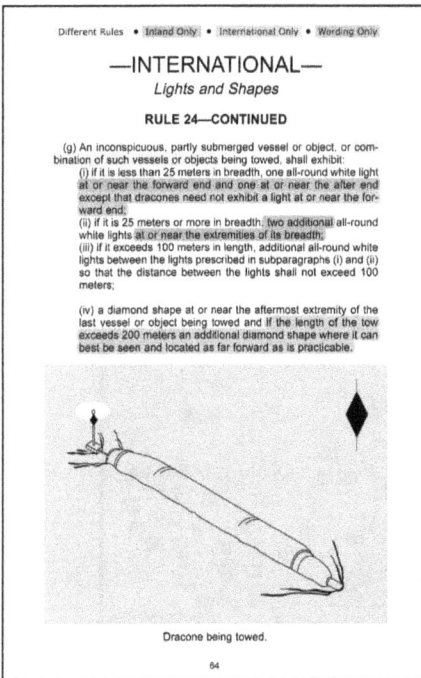

Figure 2. *This ebook publication is an exact copy of the USCG Nav Rules book, highlighted to show all differences between Inland and International Rules. Yellow is used when Inland and International have different rules; orange means it is a rule unique to Inland waters; blue means unique to International waters; and green means the wording is different but the meaning is the same.*

mail to your smartphone. Then if you are sitting around with a few minutes to spare you can ponder a few of the nuances, such as the difference between *staying clear* and *do not impede.*

One of the International Rules (Rule 1c) states that "an appropriate authority" can make rules for specific waterways that take precedence over the COLREGS. The US government has done so with what are called the US Inland Rules. These are very similar to the COLREGS in most cases, with a few important exceptions. A new ebook available online called *Annotated Navigation Rules*, highlights all the differences in an easy to interpret manner using color codes. The Canadian government has done so as well for Canadian Waters. A convenient set of the COLREGS with the Canadian modifications clearly marked in red is available as a free download at www.starpath.com/navpubs. An iPhone app for mastering the rules is described at www.navrulesmobile.com. It includes a special terms section that discusses nuances, such as noted above, close quarters, proper look out, and so on. §

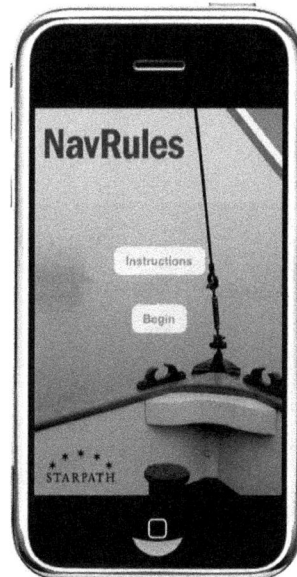

Figure 3. *This iPhone app includes a full set of the rules with related discussion, along with a quiz module that presents the full set of USCG exam questions, with answers linked to the related Rules. It includes several ways to monitor progress and to study questions related to specific rules or specific topics. Details at www.navrulesmobile.com*

TIMEKEEPING IN NAVIGATION & WEATHER

There are a dozen or so timekeeping systems used in navigation and weather, and we cannot avoid using several of them from the nav station. In the end, the main time we care about is GMT, more properly called UTC, or Universal Coordinated Time. All weather data is coordinated and reported according to UTC. In principle, we should all be calling this UTC, not GMT, but GMT is still common.

It is rather like the fact that we should all be using the metric system for these two subjects—it is in fact U.S. law that we should—but no one does, and no one complains.

Universal Coordinated Time (UTC)

UTC is the world standard time system used by all nations to coordinate weather and navigation information. It corresponds to the time used in Greenwich England for half of the year, formerly called Greenwich Mean Time. The town of Greenwich actually switches to daylight

saving time in the summer, but all scientists and navigators continue with UTC. The official UTC system (like GMT) does not employ any form of daylight saving time.

Since all weather maps and GPS information use UTC, it would seem we would want to keep our watches and ship's clocks on UTC for convenience. It turns out this is not very convenient in practice. For daily activity—at home or underway—it is much better to have our clocks reading close to what we are used to, which is often referred to as local time.

Local time, however, is a nebulous term—when used, it should always be followed up with the definition of what we mean. There are two basic times it could mean. Local time could be the local standard time or it could be the local zone time. To confuse matters a bit, local time is also sometimes used in phrases such as Pacific Time, which is intended to be Pacific Standard Time in the winter and Pacific Daylight Time in the summer—the one phrase covering both, depending on the season.

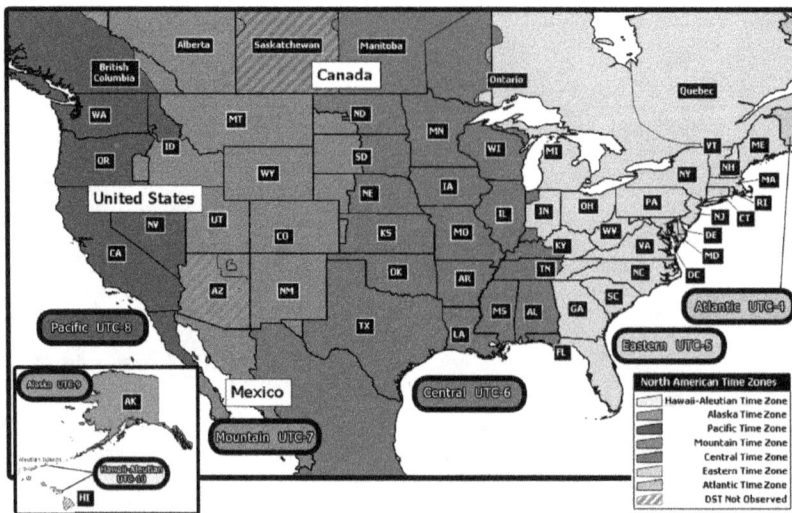

Figure 1. *North American time zones from nist.gov. That site, along with time.gov, is a good source for various aspects and history of timekeeping.*

Zone Time (ZT)

Zone time is by far the most precise of the several local times. It is the one that commercial ships and navies use when crossing an ocean— and that we all use when sitting at the USCG office taking a license exam! Zone time is determined

entirely by the longitude of your vessel at the time you record it. It will differ from UTC by a whole number of hours called the zone description (ZD).

In this time system, the world is divided into 24 time zones, each 15° wide, centered at the standard meridians, which are the longitudes that are multiples of 15 (e.g. 0, 15, 30, 45....165, 180). The borders between time zones thus take place at 7° 30′ on either side of the standard meridians.

The only exceptions are the two zones (ZD = ±12) on either side of the International Date Line, which are only 30 minutes wide (7° 30′ of longitude).

If you are keeping zone time (ZT), then you can find UTC from:

UTC = ZT + ZD, where, again, the ZD is determined by your longitude. This formula is the one that determines (or helps you remember) the sign (±) of the ZD. If your location is slow on UTC (e.g. any west longitude), then the ZD of that location is +. Eastern longitudes have negative ZDs.

To find the zone description of any particular longitude, round the longitude off to the nearest whole degree, divide by 15, and then round the result off to the nearest whole hour.

Zone time never uses daylight saving time. It is used worldwide. Zone time is never used in civilian matters; it is only for ocean navigation. One could argue that official NOAA Tide and Current Tables are given in what is essentially ZT, but we are more likely to use a reproduction of these, which converts the times to standard times.

Standard Time (EST, PST, ETC.)

Standard time is the time system used for civilian matters and for near coastal and inland navigation. Some coastal weather forecasts specify the local standard time in addition to the UTC of the report. Standard time is essentially the local zone time modified by politics and geography, and then susceptible to changes for daylight saving time.

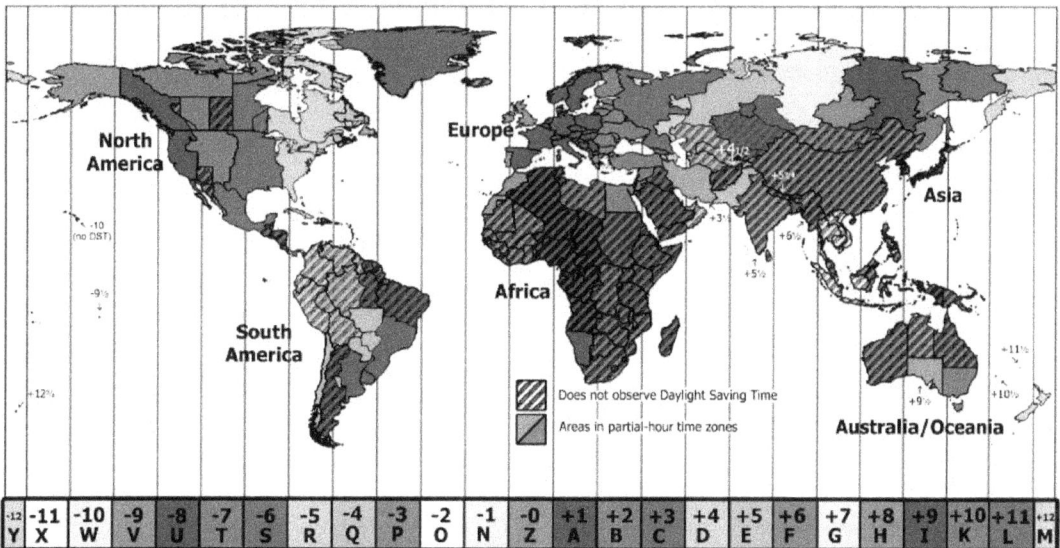

Figure 2. *Gray lines and bottom labels define zone time zones; the boundaries shown define standard time zones. Unfortunately, this nice graphic from nist.gov has the time zones labeled in the landsman's convention. The navigator's ZD of the U.S. West Coast is +8, not -8. Since Zone 0 (UTC) is labeled Z, UTC is often called zulu time, and noted (e.g. 1200z). We'll leave it to those interested in history to discover why there is no J zone (there was a reason). And if you want to ask trick questions on your navigation tests, note that ZD +12 and ZD -12 are just 30m wide, not the normal 1h.*

Standard time zones do not follow longitude lines rigorously as do the zone-time zones, but they will often be approximately along those lines, diverting to follow state and country boundaries, or maybe a river flow. We still speak of the zone descriptions of standard zones in the same way as zone times—namely, Eastern Standard Time (EST) has ZD = +5. Eastern Daylight Time would be ZD = +4, and so on. In other words, we would have UTC = EDT + 4h.

A complexity arises because standard times are often described outside of marine navigation circles as, for example, EDT being 4h behind UTC or slow on UTC. This leads to writing EDT = UTC – 4h. This is the same equation (with sides swapped), but in this line of thinking the time zone is described or labeled as -4h. Thus we often see computer and smart phone apps using reversed signs for the time zones, so we have to keep an eye out for this detail.

Watch Time (WT)

Watch time is the practical solution to time-keeping in navigation and weather. It is simply the time on your watch. To navigate by WT, I simply need to know the zone description of my watch. If I happen to have my watch set on Pacific Day light Time, that would correspond to ZD = +7. Thus, the ZD of my watch is +7 and that is all I need to know, no matter what longitude I am at as I cross the Pacific.

No matter where I am in the world, I find UTC by:

$$UTC = WT + ZD.$$

This is by far the best way to navigate, and we should always do so unless we are compelled to use ZT by labor laws, unions or some government regulation. It is easy to see that if you work day and night on ocean crossing vessels, you would want some semblance of order to your daylight and meal times, which would justify changing the ship's clocks each time you cross a time zone.

On a private vessel, however, this time changing just adds tremendous confusion to your weather and navigation. It is much better to just live with the fact that mid-day might be 2pm on your watch by the time you arrive—or you can choose to set it ahead before you leave. In other words, you go an hour or two off local time as you proceed, but that is not distracting. To minimize timekeeping errors, do not change your watch time when underway. Wait until you arrive.

Chronometer Time (CT)

For completeness, we include here also the very worst type of timekeeping—the one called Chronometer Time. This is UTC kept on a 12-hour watch face, without specifying AM or PM! Absolutely no one in the world would consider using such a time system—that is, almost no one. This is the time system used on USCG celestial navigation exams. It is the way they help support navigation schools, and we are grateful to them.

I should add that there are several forms of Universal Time and the conventions on terminology and abbreviations have not settled in yet, which is why so many folks hang onto GMT. The time that is equivalent to GMT is officially called Coordinated Universal Time, Type 1, and abbreviated UTC1, though this formal terminology is not often seen in navigation or weather resources. This is usually abbreviated as UT (*Nautical Almanac*) and UTC (NOAA weather maps). Some weather maps and forecasts also use the abbreviation Z (zulu) to mark a UTC, as we used to do for GMT. Thus, when we see a map valid at 1200Z it means 1200 UTC.

There are other time systems that have implications on navigation and weather, but only indirectly. These include the Julian Time system used by astronomers to keep track of an absolute time stamp for events in the past and future and the Solar Time system used to keep track of time relative to the time the sun crosses your meridian. The latter was used commonly in the old days of navigation, but no longer, though it still comes into play when predicting the passage times of weather satellites in sun-synchronous orbits. §

LOGBOOK PROCEDURES

Navigators and vessel owners usually have set ideas about logbooks and record-keeping underway. They vary from the most formal (pondering the notion of the ship's log as a legal document) on down to none at all (pondering... or rather, not pondering anything). A visit to Captains Nautical Supply store today found some two dozen logbook options for sale, varying from 2 x 3 inches in size to almost 2 x 3 feet in size. The preprinted forms included varied from blank lined pages to amazingly complex patterns of forms and tables to be filled in.

The choice inevitably has to be personal, but I offer here some guidelines to what has worked for me and then come back to the legal matters alluded to above. For an ocean voyage I typically have three logbooks. One is the ship's log, or deck log, which is the normal logbook referred to above. Every vessel should have one of these for all voyages and day sails. This is best done with some structured layout in a bound book. We will come back to what goes in it, and when, and why. To this basic logbook, I like to add a weather logbook and a third bound book, which could be called a notebook or a logbook.

The weather log is for transcriptions of voice broadcasts or a place to paste printed forecasts or maps, and generally a place for notes about the weather. This can be just a blank notebook. Numbered pages are nice for cross reference. Make entries sequentially from the front, and record the date at the top corner of the page. Try to avoid setting up some coded system of starting a new section in the back. Dated pages in sequence are always best. It will grow to be one of your most important books. Even on a day sail or race, you will have a set of VHF weather reporting stations you care about. You can record these in the broadcast sequence and record the reports in columns to watch how things change throughout the day. Remember the Marine Weather Service Charts explain all weather resources in your area along with their schedules (see www.starpath.com/nav-

pubs). You can also make notes on your own observations related to weather that are too specific or personal for the ship's log. It can also be the place you make a time schedule of when various reports and forecasts are available for quick reference so you don't miss any. This is a deceptively challenging task, discussed in depth in the book *Modern Marine Weather*.

The third book is a navigation journal of sorts. A place to do all general reckoning related to the navigation of the vessel. In other words, do

is time, date, position, course, and speed, entered every 4 hours or so. A more appropriate and useful log would include more columns and be entered more often.

The design we use (www.starpathpublications.com) is two-up letter size pages with 30 numbered rows. Columns on the left hand page include Date, Time, Log reading, Tack, Course (compass), Speed (knotmeter), Lat / Lon, and then 3 columns without headings for your choice of data. The usual ones I use here are COG, SOG, and WCV (waypoint closing velocity), which may have different names depending on your GPS model. In some cases you might want to change this to VMG, which is progress relative to true wind direction. The thin column for tack (P or S or M for motor) would seem redundant with the wind and course data we have, but it is still often referred to. It is best to record actual compass course and knotmeter speed (instead of just COG and SOG) because these are the data you will need to check your previous DR if you end up without GPS.

On the right-hand side we number the rows again 1 to 30 and the columns are Apparent wind speed, Apparent wind angle, Barometer, and Comments. We also ask that the person filling in the log put their initials in the Comments column or beside it. If you have true wind instruments and are confident they are working properly, you could record true wind instead of apparent.

The comments could be weather or sea state notes—these are ones related to the navigation at hand, as opposed to general matters of weather and forecasts in the weather log—sails set, when you charged the batteries, if you sight or speak another vessel, fridge or freezer temperatures, etc. Sailing anywhere near the Gulf Stream or similar currents around the world, the sea water temperature would be another key factor to log. I have never recorded or found much use for air tem-

not use scrap paper. All computations go in this book, no matter how simple—if something ends up not making sense, the paper trail can be helpful. Also record your observations and insights along the way that improve your navigation. Navigation knowledge proceeds much faster with a written record. You may learn some trick about radar tuning, or how far you can hear a buoy gong in certain sea state, etc. When you do a piloting fix there are always pertinent notes that can be added to describe it. At the end of the voyage you can then go back over what you learned. Sometimes I find these books that are 20 years old and discover when I first learned something that I now take for granted—or relearn something I had forgotten about. Though I discovered the value of this extra logbook by experience, I have since learned that the US Navy uses the Navigation Workbook (OPNAV 3530) for exactly the same purposes, so this has proven value in prudent navigation.

This book need not be for navigation alone, it could be for other matters of seamanship you picked up on the voyage. I recorded once, for example, a fantastic knot that I learned from an experienced sailor, and to this day I have never seen that knot in any other book. Again, sequential entries from the front with dated pages are best.

If you sail on a race boat with a lot of crew, boldly mark your notebooks "DO NOT USE FOR SCRAP PAPER," otherwise you will find pages torn from them at random.

The ship's log, however, is the main point at hand. The bare minimum it should include

perature outside of the Arctic, but the full picture would include the outside air temperature. Certainly if you are sailing in very high latitudes, the air temperature becomes crucial.

When to enter the log is easy. Make an entry anytime something changes. An average steered course change of 5° is a lot, and calls for an entry, as does a change of speed by a knot or so. Racing sailors tend to make an entry every hour, which is helped by the numbered rows. If not entering on the whole hour, record the time in the row with the nearest hour. This way the several watches can carry out distance made good contests per hour or per watch. When cruising it would be unlikely to enter every hour, but on any voyage the rule is at least every four hours, even if nothing changes, and if something does change make an entry. Keep in mind that if all your electronics fail, your latest logbook entry determines your navigation knowledge. In an emergency or near landfall you will be happy to have this be recent data.

You will also find that in doing weather analysis underway it is crucial to have a log entry at the synoptic times of 00, 06, 12, and 18 GMT, which are the times the weather maps are valid. Then you can compare your barometer and wind with the weather maps. You might set your watch alarm to remind you in local time when these entries should be made. Remember, too, the free service Starpath offers to provide you with live weather data at sea from ship reports. Send an otherwise blank email to shipreports@starpath. com with the word "help" in the subject line to learn about the service. With this you can get all the ship reports within 300 miles of your (or any) position over the past 6 hours. Do this an hour or so after synoptic times to check your barometer and weather maps. You can also read about this at www.starpath.com/barometers.

If you are on a route to a foreign port in a vessel of any size, or your vessel is over 100 T in local waters, then 46 USC §11301 (ecfr.gpoaccess.gov) explains the legal requirements for logbooks, which are indeed rather elaborate, though the regulations are addressed mostly to safety issues, along with the makeup and behavior of the crew. Specific types of vessels have specific logbook entry requirements, although navigation entries are not addressed. Logbook procedures for Sailing School Vessels, for example, are covered in CFR 46 §169.841. We learn from all these required procedures that we might want to include in our non-required logbooks a couple of pages to list:

• Departure and destination

• Documentation or registration number of the vessel

• Draft of the vessel

• Names and nationalities of all crew members. (If you are sailing into foreign waters you should also know if any has been convicted of a crime.)

• List of the safety drills and inspections you have carried out, station bills established, and a statement that all crew members have been in-

formed of the safety procedures on board.

Furthermore, it is not really an option as we learn from 46 CFR §78.37-3, Part (b): "The master or person in charge of a vessel that is not required by 46 U.S.C. 11301 to have an official logbook, shall maintain, on board, an unofficial logbook or record in any form desired for the purposes of making entries therein as required by law or regulations in this subchapter. Such logs or records... must be kept available for review by a marine inspector for a period of 1 year after the date to which the records refer."

I must admit that I have never sailed on an ocean passage in a yacht where these data were specifically included as part of the ship's log, but the virtue of the addition is clear in the event there were an accident. It could also be helpful in some port operations in foreign waters. On the other hand, there have been many times I wished in retrospect that we had kept a list of the crew members we sailed with on specific voyages. These records can also be valuable to crew members who one day want to apply for a USCG deck license, as this book can then help document their sea time.

You might also want to start a logbook numbering sequence for your vessel, so that as you sail more there is an order to your sequence of logbooks. The USCG offers a free copy of their Merchant Marine Official Logbook for those who are required to carry one. It is called CG 706B. It contains much information and references, but it is not very useful for small-craft deck logs. The master or owner of a sailing vessel on international routes may want to request one and read the official requirements. If you are playing Nautical Pursuit and need this answer, this is the place you will find the phrase "the ship's logbook is a legal document," but admiralty attorneys will still remind us that this is an imprecise phrase. §

Sample pages from the Starpath Sailor's Logbook

	Date	Time	Log	Course	Speed	Location	
1							
2							
3							
4							
5							
6							
7							
8							
9							
10							
11							
12							
13							
14							
15							
16							
17							
18							
19							
20							
21							
22							
23							
24							
25							
26							
27							
28							
29							
	1	2	3	4	5	6	7

	AWS	AWA	Baro	Comments
1				
2				
3				
4				
5				
6				
7				
8				
9				
10				
11				
12				
13				
14				
15				
16				
17				
18				
19				
20				
21				
22				
23				
24				
25				
26				
27				
28				
29				
	8	9	10	11

COMPASS CHECKS WITH THE SUN

This shortcut method of accurate compass checking works on sunny days for binnacle-mounted compasses on non-steel boats that have a shadow pin in the center—most do, although they are often overlooked. A shadow pin is a vertical pin about an inch tall mounted in the center of the card. The pin is there as a guide to taking bearings, as well as for use with the sun, as explained in this article. This method can be used on any waters—even in confined docking areas (turning the boat with lines)—and does not require a chart, knowledge of the local magnetic variation, nor any special knowledge of celestial navigation.

Shadow Bearing

When the sun shines across the card, the pin casts a shadow on it, and the bearing of this shadow can be used as a reference for compass checks. This method is best used in early morning or late afternoon, when the sun is low enough so that the shadow reaches the numbers on the perimeter of the compass card. When the sun is higher, the shadow is short and you must use a ruler and some patience to project the line of the shadow out to the numbers. In any event, you need to read this shadow bearing as accurately as possible, which with a little practice in calm conditions is about 1° precision, even on cards marked only every 5°.

Although the magnetic bearing of the sun changes continuously throughout the day as it moves westward across the sky, the change is slow enough in most cases to assume that it is constant over a period of a few minutes. And that is all it takes to swing ship and check the sun's bearing as you go around. If there is no error in the compass (no deviation), then the shadow bearing will be the same regardless of the boat's heading. With

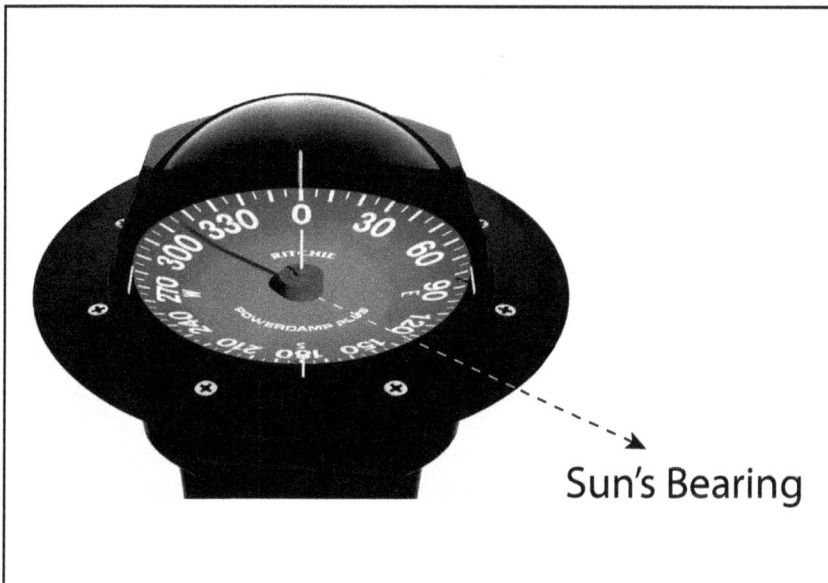

Figure 1. *With a little practice, this method can be used anywhere your sails take you.*

deviation in the compass, the shadow bearing will be different on different headings, and this difference can be used to determine the deviation on any heading.

Checking the Compass

On non-steel hulls, it is usually adequate to check the compass only on the cardinal compass headings (N, S, E and W). If these are right, you can be confident that the intermediate headings are also correct. The procedure is to head north according to the compass. Read the shadow's bearing from the compass card and record it; then proceed around to the left or right, reading the shadow bearing while holding steady compass courses on E, S, W and N again.

The second shadow bearing headed north should be the same as it was when you started if you got around in time. If off a degree or two, it won't matter for this first check to see what the overall errors look like. The second approximation used in this method it that any errors you find will be equal and opposite on reciprocal compass headings. Translated into practical terms, this means that if the shadow bearing was 250° when headed north and 270° when headed south, its proper bearing should have been 260° on both headings. In other words, your compass read 10° low when headed north (deviation 10° east) and 10° high when headed south (deviation 10° west).

Recording Deviations and Removing Errors

With any deviation in the compass, the errors you find in the north-south direction must be different from the ones you find in the east-west direction. In the last example, you might have also found that when headed east, the shadow bearing was 255° (dev 5° E) and when headed west, it was 265° (dev 5° W). The N-S errors must be removed from the compass separately from the E-W errors.

In many cases, it is adequate for navigation to simply record these deviations and correct for them as needed. To remove the errors with the internal adjustment magnets, first do another check of the N and S errors. From this, you can figure out what the proper shadow bearing should be now

that some time has passed. The 10° error should be the same if the measurements were good, but the bearings will be centered on a slightly different value; say by now, at 265°, meaning that you actually read 275° and 255°. Head north on the compass and pick a reference mark (or star) to steer toward during the adjustment. Use either of the side screws (running athwartships through the compass) to shift the compass heading 10°. The compass was low on a north heading, so you would turn the adjustment screw until your heading read 010°, without altering the actual heading of the boat. To double check the direction, watch the shadow bearing; it should move to 265° as you adjust the card.

This will be a very small turn of the screw, just a few degrees rotation typically, and generally the direction is toward "neutral" on the adjustment magnets, meaning toward a direction that makes the screw slots more parallel to the waterline. The adjustments must be made with a nonmagnetic screwdriver, or with the brass key provided with many compasses for this purpose.

Next, re-measure the E-W errors, because correcting the N-S errors could have changed the E-W values. This is especially likely if the errors you removed were over 15° or so. Then remove the E-W errors in the same manner, but this time head east or west and use the fore or aft adjusting screw.

Some French and English compasses do not have internal magnets for this adjustment. These compasses typically have empty tubes lying along each side of the compass, into which separate magnets must be inserted for compensation. This job is best done by a professional, as it will take more time and money to track down the right magnets to use than it will cost to have someone do it for you.

The method described here is a back-up for the more precise method of using the actual numerical value of the sun's true bearing (Zn), which can be computed by standard celestial navigation techniques. This more accurate method requires knowing your Lat and Lon, the correct GMT, and the local magnetic variation. §

OPEN SOURCE NAVIGATION

Electronic charting is not new. There have been many fine commercial echart programs on the market for very many years, decades even. You might think it is new, based on terminology we see. Terminology and conventions are actually still evolving.

And there are indeed still ongoing significant developments in this important area of navigation. We covered "Wrinkles in ESC" (electronic charting systems) in the January column, which makes a good background for this one. For some time now there has been a new kid on the block that is slowly becoming better known in nav stations and pilothouses around the world—still a bit in the category of "Well known to those who know it well," but not for long.

OpenCPN is an open source echart program that first appeared in 2008 to a few select users, but it is now a full fledged, multi-functional tool used worldwide. As is the virtue of open source software, it is still evolving. It may not have all the polished edges of its commercial counterparts, but it is an excellent full-function tool that makes a great back up to your favorite commercial product. See www.opencpn.org for details and download.

Since it is a free product, it offers an ideal way for mariners to get their feet wet on ECS before buying a commercial product, some of which are a big investment. And it has a lot of unique virtues on its own. For example, it has a broad array of chart options it can display, including both RNC (raster navigation charts) and ENC (electronic navigation charts). The former, most popularly in the BSB format, are static graphic images of the existing NOAA paper charts. The latter are vector products, most popularly in the S-57 format. Vector "charts" are just text files that tell the echart program how to draw the chart on the screen. They have tremendous versatility and in principle can include much more information, but this science is still a work in progress—at least in my mind as navigator and navigation teacher.

You can get both types of charts for US waters at no charge from NOAA. To save time, start at www.starpath.com/getcharts. In each case, click the Name of the chart set you want, and then at the bottom of the long agreement form there is an OK link that goes to the charts.

To learn more about the program, there is a sub-forum on www.cruisersforum.com called Navigation/OpenCPN. It is a good place to keep up with developments and to ask questions. The program's originator and Lead Developer David Register (signing in as "bdbcat") takes part, as well as do other developers and many users, worldwide. Richard Smith and David Herring are co-developers of the Mac version.

There are numerous OpenCPN plugins and supplements available or in the works, offered from third party developers—again, a beauty of the open source format. The GRIB weather display function is still very basic, but it is underway and it will show GFS GRIBS from any source. Some other supplements I tested seem still under development—or at least the instructions are under development.

One feature that already works well is the display of tides and currents for any location on the chart. This is not a surprise; if you skim the list of co-developers you will find the name of Dave Flatner, who has set the standard in this topic worldwide with work on his own program XTide.

Another impressive utility we learn about from the OpenCPN folks is how to make georeferenced BSB echarts from any image you view on Google Earth. This procedure is not unique to OpenCPN—it was developed by Paul Higgins (www.gdayii.ca)—but the fact that it is so openly discussed and supported in the OpenCPN community is a reflection on the open source attitude of the developers and users. I made a sample nautical chart of Wordon Pond, RI this way. Such a chart can be shown and navigated on in OpenCPN or you can transfer it to an iPhone app

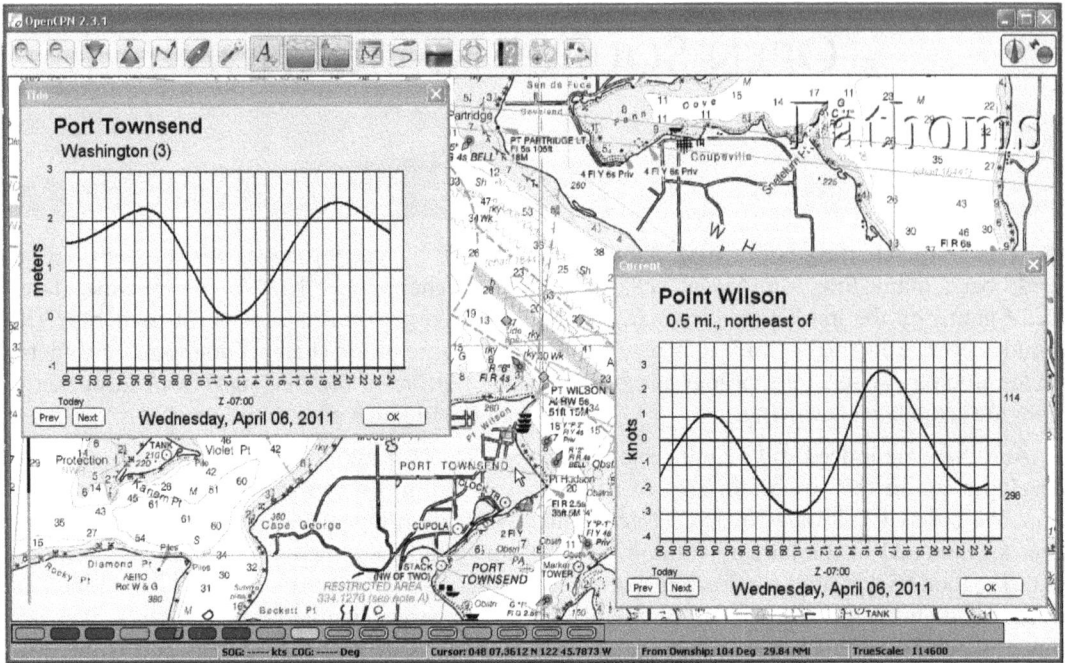

Figure 1. *Tide and current display from OpenCPN software.*

like Memory Map to practice navigation in your canoe on the lake.

One feature that very definitely marks this as new in the world of echarts is the near identical program for both the PC and the Mac. This is something new in all programming. Before the iPhone, there were not many mariners using Macs, but these days you find many folks with both types of computers, and they are happy to have tools they can use on both. And there is, of course, a linux version for computer purist sailors.

Standard features one might expect these days are all there, including GPX input and output so you can transfer routes, tracks, and other data between Google Earth and OpenCPN, as well as AIS reception and display. The manuals also teach how to make georeferenced echarts from graphic images of maps or satellite photos. To drive the point home, they provide georeferenced Pilot Charts that load just as any echart would. These are excellent for route planning. You can also georeference weather maps with their tools for convenient weather routing decisions.

Missing according to my style of navigation is the ability to tile the screen so we can simultane-

ously see both large scale and small scale views of our position. We can watch our track zoomed way in to spot set and drift, and from the smaller scale display we can identify what we see on the horizon—the little picture and the big picture. This tiling is also often valuable for comparing a vector rendering of the corresponding paper chart. This is always an informative exercise. I am told this tiling option is on the active wish list of new features.

Figure 1. *Georeferenced Google Earth image viewed in OpenCPN.*

One feature of OpenCPN that appeals to me is its policy of sticking as much as possible to the standard ECDIS display format for the S-57 vector charts. Several commercial companies seem to argue (maybe even rightfully) that the ECDIS standards are too cumbersome and could be improved, so they just improve them. This is a mixed blessing. There is definitely a virtue in using international standards on chart symbols and notation. This has been, I believe, well achieved in paper chart notation, and we have the booklet *Chart No. 1* as a guide to the meanings.

Unfortunately, there is no real counterpart to this booklet for the ENC. There is an appendix to an IHO document (International Hydrographic Office) that is called "Chart No. 1," but this is really stretching the point. Besides conventions in graphic symbols there are also conventions on what should be charted and how it should be described. In S-57 charting, much of the information about an object is obtained by right clicking it and reading the text. In fact, there is not even consistency in the name. In this official IHO document, they use both S57 and S-57, and many others mix these up at random. The proper name is with the dash (S-57) according to the US representative to the IHO, so one starting point is to get that right so we can use search engines, etc.

And just to show the challenge in front of us, the IHO document that explains the symbology of S-57 format is called "S-52." There are historic reasons for that apparently, but still, our work is cut out for us. So seeing a conventional ECDIS output in the OpenCPN is a nice starting point. It can help us interpret the ENC that we see in other echart programs. As it is now, you can download an S-57 chart from NOAA and the symbols might look quite different on different echart programs. Recall that one contributing factor to the allision of the *Cosco Busan* with the Bay Bridge was the pilot's confusion of chart symbols on an echart display he was not familiar with—why he did not have a smart phone or PDA in his pocket with ECS he knew well is another question.

I look forward to learning more about the S-57 conventions and we will post what we learn at www.starpath.com/navpubs. There are already several references there for paper charts and for S-57 echarts. §

INLAND &
COASTAL
NAVIGATION

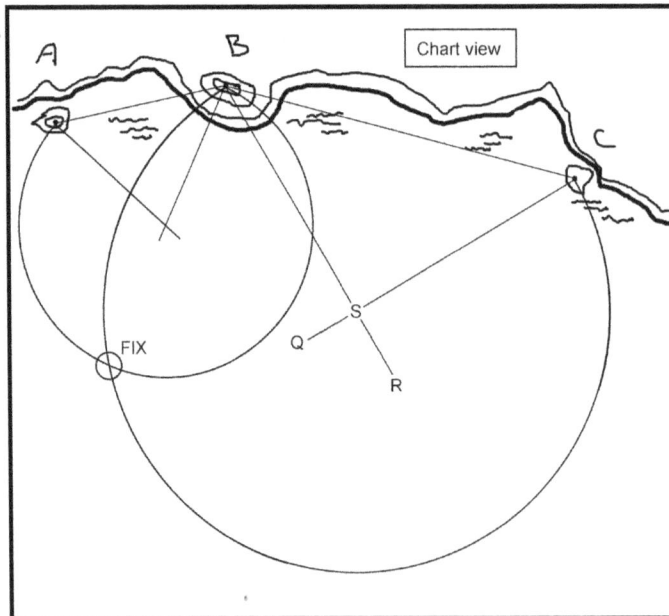

WRINKLES IN PRACTICAL ECS

The use of ECS (Electronic Chart Systems) is fundamental to modern navigation, just as much as it is fundamental that we know how to navigate without it. The term means connecting a GPS to an echart display and navigating by moving map technology. An icon representing the boat shows where you are at all times on an electronic version of a nautical chart. You can view the chart in dedicated echart plotters or in the chart display of a GPS unit, or in your smart phone, but the most functionality comes with viewing the charts in a PC program dedicated to the task, running in a laptop.

The acronym ECDIS (Electronic Chart Display and Information System) means essentially the same thing, but it refers to the official system of the International Maritime Organization (IMO) that has strict standards on the types of charts, the hardware, and the format of the display. Ships must use ECDIS; yachts can use anything they like and call it ECS.

The types of GPS units and the types of echart display devices we can choose from are changing rapidly. A blue tooth GPS running one of several excellent programs in a small laptop offers excellent mobility if you sail on different boats. The full package including a few custom echarts is around $900 or so.

Some one dozen years ago, when we were asked "Should I take a computer along on my cruise?" the answer was if you need one for your work and entertainment, then Yes, but otherwise the hassle might not be worth the reward in navigation and communication. Now if we get the same question, the answer is No, you should not take a computer along, you should take two. Build two of these laptops with all of your navigation, communications, and weather software

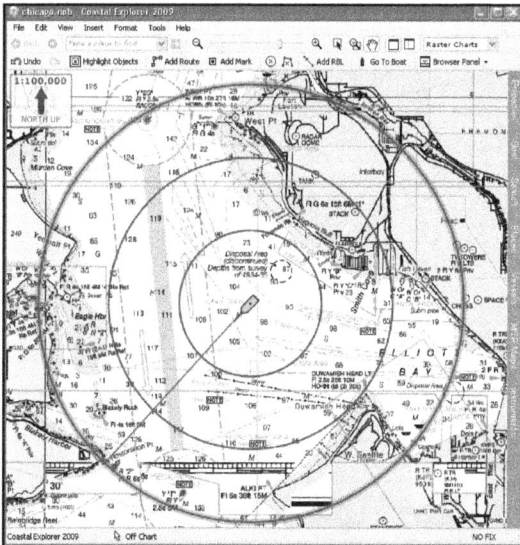

Figure 1. *Echart display with range rings on vessel icon set to match those on the radar for a quick ID of the targets and our relative location. Notice the unambiguous dah-dit radar signal of the RACON just aft of the starboard beam, nicely collaborated with the echart rings. Echart from Coastal Explorer. Radar image from* Radar for Mariners. *The fourth ring showing on the radar is a variable range marker, being pulled into position with the plus-sign cursor.*

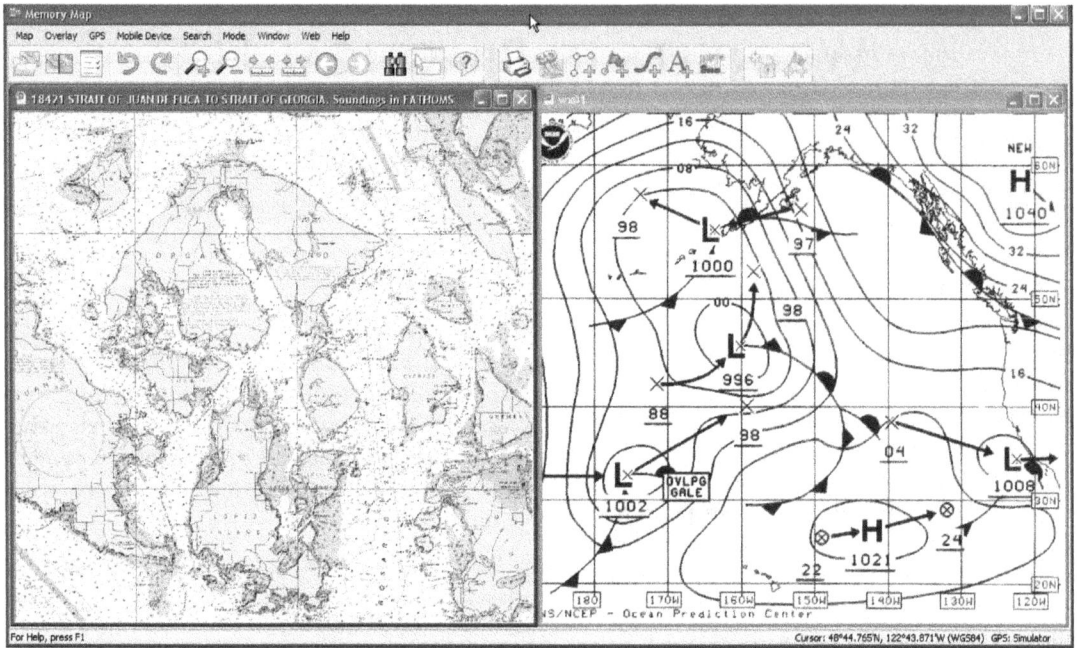

Figure 2. *Echart programs such as Memory-Map Navigator can georeference weather maps and pilot charts for direct on map navigation. This program also comes in a Mobile PC and iPhone application.*

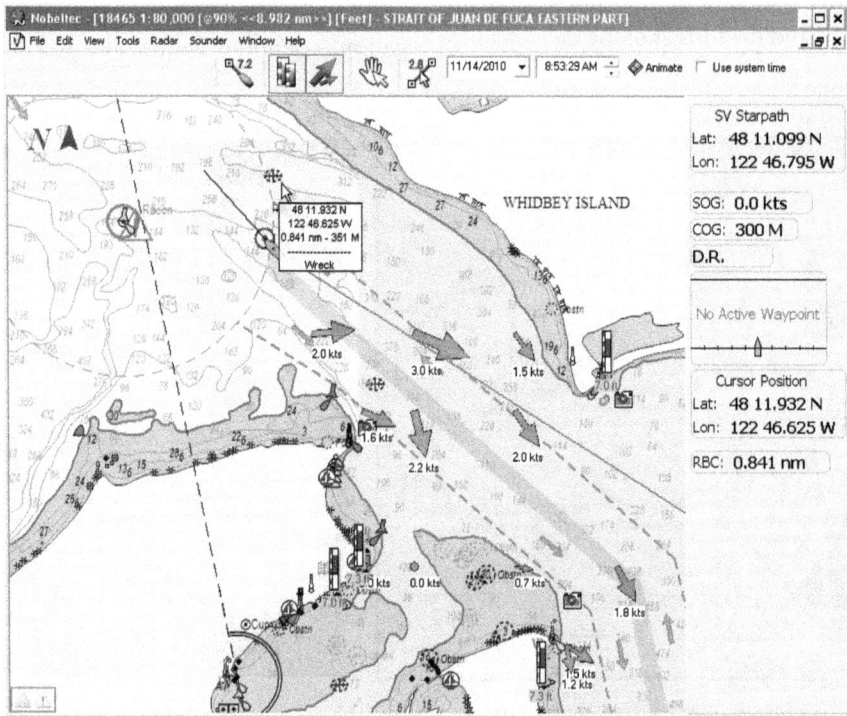

Figure 3. *Nobeltec's Visual Navigation Suite has very convenient tide and current displays, which can be further enhanced with a click to present the data as graphs or tables. This program and several others will also allow for navigating on georeferenced satellite or aerial photos.*

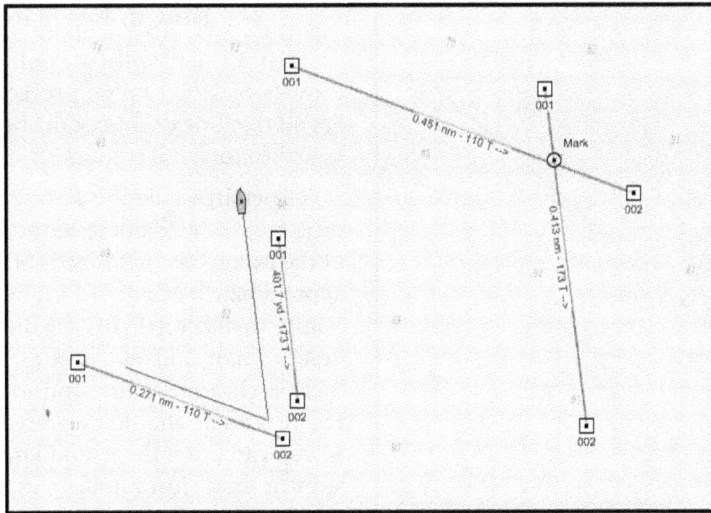

Figure 4. *ECS is the best way to call the layline in strong current or leeway. Assuming things stay the same, once you have tacked and get your tracks on each board you can plot bearing lines to match them and move them to the mark, then figure the best route and time to the laylines. If the track is no longer parallel to what you started with, then something has changed: wind or current, or helm.*

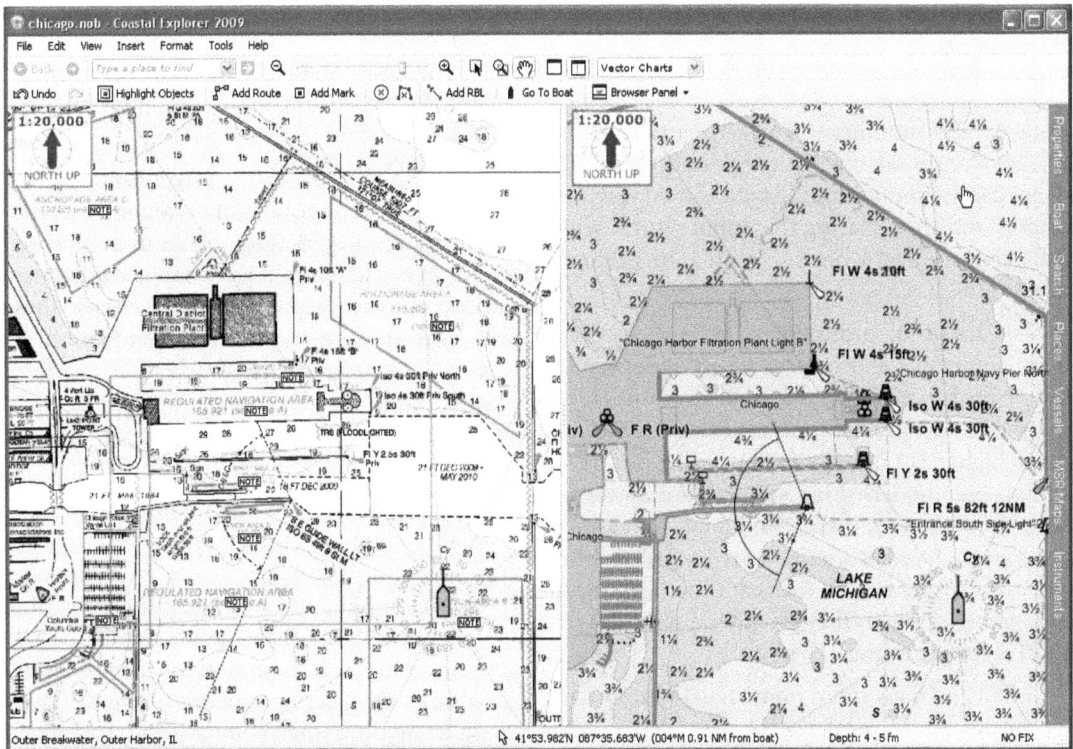

Figure 5. *RosePoint's Coastal Explorer can display both the bitmap raster navigation charts (RNC) and the vector electronic navigation charts (ENC) both available at no charge from NOAA for US waters. When both are available you will find times when one is preferred over the other, for varying reasons.*

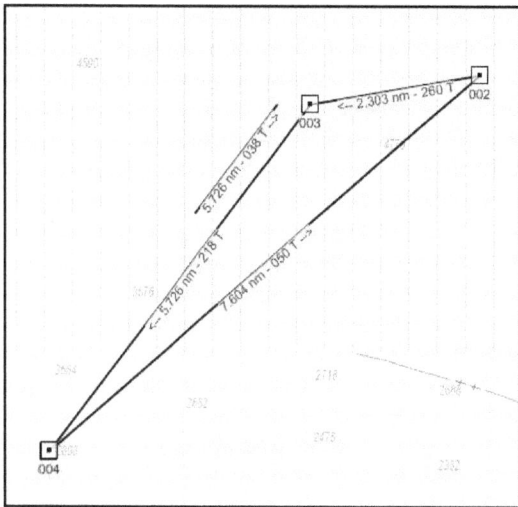

Figure 6. *ESC programs are very convenient for solving vector problems in navigation. A simple example is shown. Steering 050T at 7.6 kts, what will we make good in current of 2.3 kts at 260 T? At any location on any chart, make a 3-leg route of the vector triangle for a one hour period, then reverse the last leg to learn is is SMG=5.73 at CMC=038. Even the most complex vector problems are easily solved in this manner.*

installed and running, so you have a mirror image back up. It takes some tweaking to get a PC dependably communicating with several external devices and then sharing this input with several programs running at once, so there is no point in doing it twice.

The hassle of protecting a PC and its even more vulnerable attachments when underway in the ocean has not changed at all over the years, but the reward you get from the system is so very much higher. For now we are discussing just navigation, but modern high seas communications and weather data gathering and analysis requires a computer. Needless to say, there are sailors who successfully sail around the world without these aids, but in doing so they give up tremendous resources for safety and efficiency.

ECS is perhaps more immediately important on inland and coastal waters, but even in the ocean the same basic procedures and advantages apply. Here is a brief outline, which we might call...

How to Navigate Today

Step 1. Start with waypoints. Every voyage, 2 miles or 2,000 miles, proceeds by waypoints. Spend the time to choose the best way to go, taking all factors into account.

Generally we do this selection with the echart program, zoomed out to see an overview of most of the route. Use the route tool to quickly set the approximate location of each of the main turning points, then zoom in to drag the waypoints to the best position, and add more as needed. Then give them each a real name and lock their position. The real name should be preceded by a number, so you can order them, and know where you are along a route. Just numbers or just names is not good.

Then make a printed voyage plan table or spread sheet with the names and lat, lon of each point, and the course and distance between them. Also add estimated speeds for each leg of the route. Most echart programs will format this data for you and figure the times at each way point and then export or print this record directly for you. Somehow we should end up with a printed record. We are dealing with computers after all, and we don't want to do this twice.

For inland waters, the waypoints are best when in view of a prominent radar target, or other way to uniquely identify the location by visual means. In broad terms, it is the job of a good navigation course to teach you how to choose these waypoints. It is the key step in the navigation.

If you are planning for a yacht race, or if any part of your cruising voyage calls for crucial navigation, then I would immediately export these waypoints from the PC program into your hand-held GPS. It takes some instructions manual reading to learn the process of transferring waypoints, routes, or actual tracts between PC and hand-held, but well worth it. If anything goes wrong at a crucial moment, you will then be ready instantly with a solution. As navigator, you can also be monitoring progress along the route as you sit on deck when you have your hand-held programmed.

Then the job is to follow the waypoints. If you cut corners or skip waypoints then the set up was wrong. There will be discoveries along the way that call for waypoint changes, but if so, change the waypoint and then sail the waypoints you now have. Remember, you might be sailing the route again someday, so you can record it properly now for the next time. In a sense, if you do not follow the waypoints you are not navigating; you are just sailing there.

Step 2. Successive waypoints define the line between them. Our job is to stay on that line to the very best we can. When under sail, we will have obvious limitations on our route, but we still must keep that line in mind at all times. Let's look at the simplest case first, under power or reaching so we have control over our heading.

Leaving the first waypoint, head the boat in the direction of the next waypoint, say it is 300 M, and steer that course as accurately as you can for some time, and watch your track on the echart—the breadcrumb trail of your past positions.

"Watching the track" is usually done best with a dual display of the same chart. Open a second window showing the boat and zoom one display in and the other display out. The close view can show within boat lengths if you wander off the desired track to the next waypoint. The far view keeps you in perspective of where you are along the route.

Step 3. If you see you are getting set, meaning your actual track is diverging from the desired course line for any reason (we do not care what is causing it), then it is a call for action. Zoomed way in it will be obvious in short time provided you are steering a steady course. The navigator needs the helmsman's help at this stage. If the COG is 315M, for example, as you steer and desire to make good 300M, then you are "getting set" 15° to the right. We speak of this in water currents terminology, but it is actually an "error current," whose source is not important at this stage. It could just as well be due to a compass error as to moving water.

To correct for this offset, turn left "into the current" by this 15° and watch your COG and track again. If you are now making good 300, then fine, if not, tweak the heading till you get exactly what you want. Suppose you find that steering 283 puts you right on a COG of 300, so now you are tracking along the chart precisely parallel to your desired line. At this stage it is best to over-correct (steer 260) for as long as it takes to get back on

your actual track line, then come back to 283 and all is right in the world. You are tracking straight down your line. Then keep an eye on your track and adjust as needed. At the next waypoint turn to the new course and do it all again.

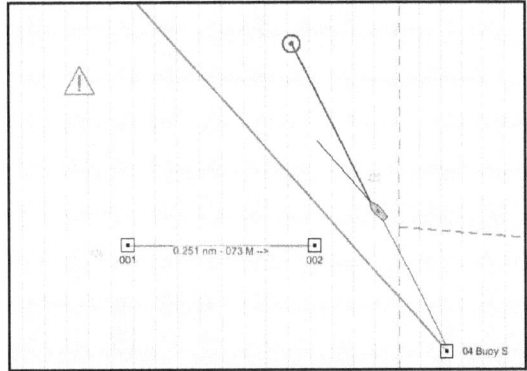

Step 3-1. *Spot the set. The red line is the course to next mark at 300M. Knotmeter speed is 6 kts. A current of about 2 kts is flowing N-NE, causing a set of about 15°. The black line on the vessel icon is the heading line (at 300M), the blue line shows the COG (at 315M) and predicted location of the boat in 2 minutes. Notice that in less than 2 minutes we have a good idea of our set when zoomed in to this scale.*

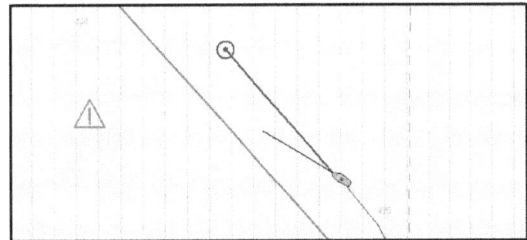

Step 3-2. *Correct the course and check the results. After turning into the current by 15° (to heading 285M), we find we need a bit more correction and 283 M tracks parallel to the desired course with COG = 300M.*

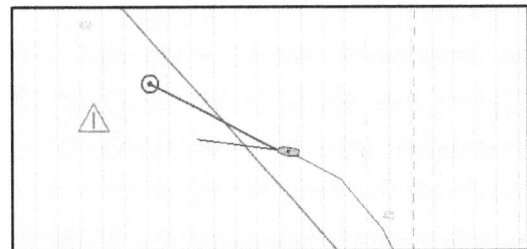

Step 3-3. *Over correct (heading = 260M) to get back on desired track. Making good the right course is not enough. We want to make good the right course in the right place.*

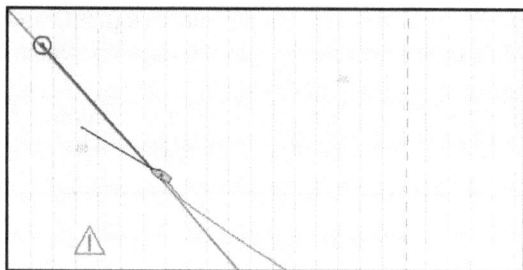

Step 3-4. *Once back on the track, we can turn to the proper course that we know corrects for current, namely 283M, and we are now tracking right down the line as desired. It is easy to do. We should not except less.*

Step 4. The hallmark of good navigation is not relying on any single navigation aid, and that includes GPS. A versatile ECS can implement quick checks of your GPS position and rate of travel. Radar and depth sounder are often the first instruments to check.

Using raster echarts (graphic images of paper charts, called RNC), you can read or interpolate the depth at your position from the printed soundings, correct for tide height, and compare it with your depth sounder. Or easier still, note when the echart display shows you crossing a prominent ledge within soundings, and watch to see the depth sounder confirm the crossing. This method is less sensitive to your sounder's calibration. Vector echarts on the other hand, since they are rendered images of digitized chart data (called ENC), can actually compute and display the charted depth at your location to compare with your depth sounder. Many echart programs include digital tide predictions, which expedite the process.

Several echart programs allow the user to set multiple range rings on the vessel icon. This is a very handy feature. You can set these range rings to match the range rings on your present radar display and also set the display mode (head-up or north-up) to match, and then use the echart display for an instant interpretation of the radar screen. This comparison is one of the best ways possible to confirm your position—or when disoriented, it is a quick way to regain what is formally called "situational awareness," a worthy goal at all times, on the water and off.

When all radar targets are clearly identified, we can get by for position checks just using the range and bearing to good radar targets. Both values are obtained digitally from the radar and the ECS display. Without radar, compass bearings can be used, or better still an inexpensive plastic sextant for quick, very accurate fixes as described in the Oct, 2010 issue.

Another tool of most echart programs that can expedite safe efficient navigation is the predictor line that can be set on the vessel icon. This line shows the instantaneous direction of the COG, along with marking where you will be at some preset time interval. The time projection can be minutes or hours, depending on the circumstances, but it is almost always a valuable addition to the display.

A few more ECS procedures are shown in the pictures here. These include choosing the layline with current and leeway, and solving any type of standard navigation vector problems. Most echart programs offer a free demo version, some of which can be used indefinitely with limitations. Echarts of US waters are free these days from NOAA, so it free and easy to learn the ropes of ECS to discover which system best meets your needs. §

READ THE CHART!

We often think of chart reading as the process of interpreting the symbols and perspective of a nautical chart. There are several aspects of the process. It is takes some practice, for example, to see the three-dimensional world from the two-dimensional presentation on a flat chart. Experience with topo maps is helpful. We also learn that the vast array of symbols used must be interpreted carefully. The notations (6), (6), and (6), for example, have dramatically different meanings when describing the adjacent rock symbol.

The main resource that explains chart symbols and abbreviations is called *Chart No. 1*. This is a strange name because it is a booklet, not a chart, but at least all members of the International Hydrographic Organization (www.iho.int) use the same name for the corresponding resource for their charts. If you are planning to sail into foreign waters, use this site to track down charting resources.

But that is not the kind of chart reading I am talking about for now. I am talking about literally reading the chart. Besides all the graphics and symbols, there is a lot of text on the chart, usually on the land parts. When you get a new chart it is extremely valuable to take out a few minutes to read all text on the chart. Map out some systematic way to cover all sections, to insure not missing any notes. There are many interesting things to learn, more on some charts than others.

First of all, your focused reading of a new chart means you will not overlook the date of the chart and the units of the soundings, feet or fathoms. Some years ago there was a ruling passed that all charts were to move to meters by a specific date and sure enough NOAA started printing a meters version on the back sides of all charts to help us transition into the change. But the due date came and went, and no one complained, so the ruling was quietly forgotten. Now with no money it is a non-issue.

Old charts might also be in an old horizontal datum (such as NAD 27), in which case you would have to set your GPS to that datum for accurate work. This is pretty much history now when using new charts. New charts are all at WGS 84 which is the GPS default setting.

Sometimes a chart will include references to information from the corresponding Marine Weather Service Chart (MSC) telling the local NOAA VHF weather radio channels and their range of reception. See link to MSC online at www.starpath.com/navpubs.

One thing that is always there are the values of mean high water (MHW) for various regions of the chart. You might guess this is information we would get from Tide Tables, but that is not the case. This crucial information is only on the charts. Recall that charted depths (soundings)

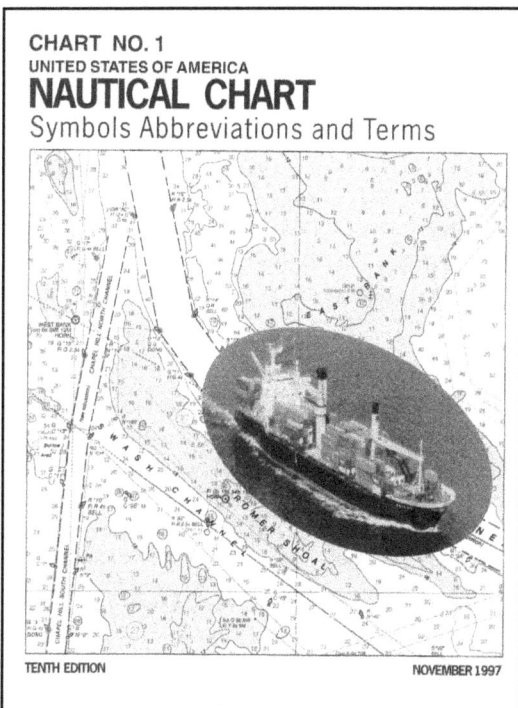

CHART NO. 1
UNITED STATES OF AMERICA
NAUTICAL CHART
Symbols Abbreviations and Terms

TENTH EDITION   NOVEMBER 1997

Figure 1. *Chart No. 1.*

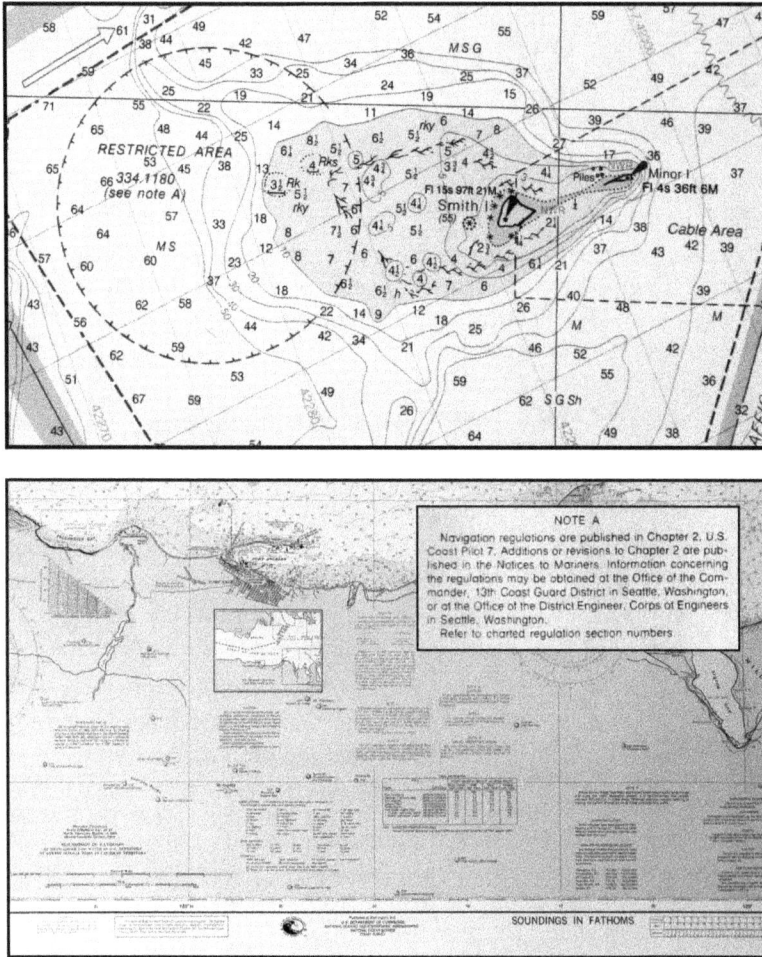

Figure 2. *Restricted Area, see Note A.*

are given relative to zero tide height, the times of which we do get from tide books, but elevations of land and clearances under bridges are all given relative to MHW. It is an important number to know. If a bridge clearance is listed as 50 ft and the tide at the moment is 2 ft, with a MHW of 8 ft for this region, then you have a clearance of 56 ft at the moment. Only when the tide is higher than MHW do you have less clearance than stated.

Sometimes we see chart notes reminding us of standard symbol distinctions that might be important on this chart, such as circle with a dot is an accurate location, whereas a smaller circle without a dot is an approximate location.

Text on the chart will also remind you of which Coast Pilot volume applies to the charted region. Recall that the broad task of these publications is to provide crucial navigational in-

formation that is not included on the chart. The various labeled caution areas and restricted areas on a chart are usually explained in the associated Coast Pilot. Coast Pilots are online in full form (linked at www.starpath.com/navpubs).

It can be very informative to look up the details of the posted restricted areas, i.e. How is it restricted? Why is this area restricted? These explanations are often not given on the chart itself, and if you do not read the chart you will not know how to find the answer. Not far from us here in Seattle we have one listed as "RESTRICTED AREA 334.1180 see Note A."

Note A tells us to find the answer in Chapter 2 of the Coast Pilot. What the chart does not tell us, and what our standard reference *Chart No. 1* does not tell us as well, is that the number listed is a reference to the US Code of Federal Regulations (CFR) that specifies this restriction. Check the sidebar here to see that this is clearly very important information.

If you do not have a Coast Pilot, knowing what the number means might let you look it up online with your cell phone. Find the CFRs online at ecfr.gpoaccess.gov. The titles related to navigation are 33 and 46. If you have a laptop on your vessel there is no reason not to have these at hand, along with a copy of the Coast Pilot, as well as the Navigation Rules, and Light List. These are fundamental references we should have onboard along with the tide and current tables.

To master the other type of chart reading and related navigational matters, have a look at the interactive Starpath Chart Trainer software program. It is a sophisticated electronic version of Chart No.1 and other resources, as well as a training tool in the use of nautical charts. §

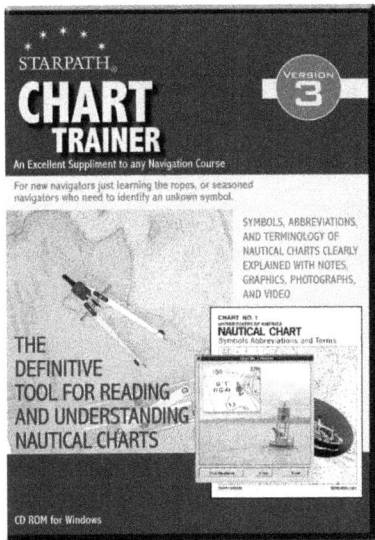

Figure 4. *Starpath Chart Trainer Software.*

§334.1180 Strait of Juan de Fuca, WA; air-to-surface weapon range, restricted area.

(a) The restricted area.

A circular area immediately west of Smith Island with a radius of 1.25 nautical miles having its center at latitude 48° 19' 11" North and longitude 122° 54' 12" West. In the center of the area will be located a lighted and radar reflective buoy to serve as a navigational aid to mariners. The area will be used for air-to-surface target practice using non-explosive training devices.

(b) The regulations.

(1) No person, vessel or other watercraft shall enter or remain within the designated restricted area between 0700 and 1200 hours daily, local time except as authorized by the enforcing agency and as follows: The area will be open to commercial gill net fishing during scheduled fishing periods from June 15 to October 15, annually. The October 15 closure date will be extended by the enforcing agency if determined as advantageous to the commercial gill net fishing by the Washington State Department of Fisheries.

(2) Prior to each target practice operation the restricted area will be patrolled by naval aircraft. Those persons and vessels found within the restricted area will be overflown by the aircraft at an altitude of not less than 300' in the direction in which the unauthorized person and vessel are to proceed to clear the area.

(c) The regulations in this section shall be enforced by the Commandant, Thirteenth Naval District, Seattle, Washington, and such agencies as he may designate

PROGRESS TO WEATHER

The key to long term success in navigation is good DR (dead reckoning). In its broadest sense it means figuring the best estimate of your present and future positions (without piloting or electronic aids) using all other information available to you.

Your log and compass readings are the starting points, but then there are many corrections and adjustments to make, not the least of which are tied to the strength and direction of the wind.

Strong persistent head winds bring a new twist to navigation that has a serious affect on DR if not accounted for. Three factors that don't matter much in light air now matter a lot. These are wind-driven current, helm bias, and leeway. They are each fairly small effects, even in strong winds, but they all cause error in the same direction, so their sum is not small. They cause navigational error because they are invisible—they take us off course and we have no way of knowing it until the next position fix. In short, we must simply make an educated guess of their individual sets and drifts and correct our DR accordingly.

Leeway is how much a boat slips to leeward on a windward course. It is a function of the boat's draft, the point of sail, and the wind speed. It's only a navigational factor when going to weather close hauled in strong winds—or very light wind, but that is not the subject here. The effect is distinctly different from current set because we can measure leeway underway (without electronics in some cases), so it is not strictly invisible as implied above. A typical keel boat of 6-foot draft might slip as much as 10° to leeward in a solid 15 knots of true wind. Yacht design specs might have this number as just a few degrees, but here

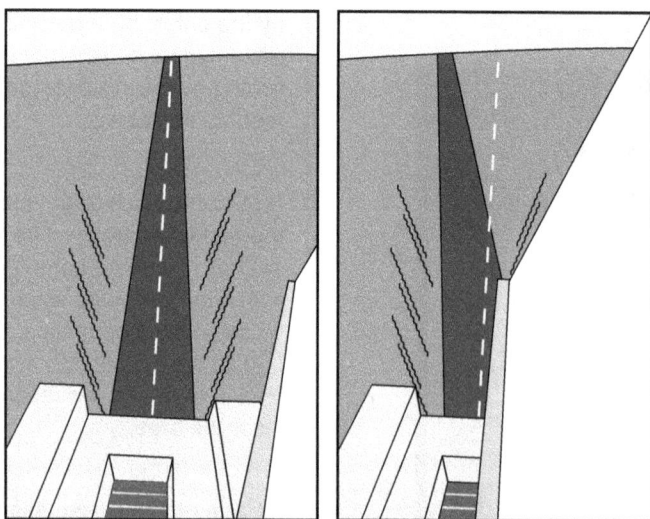

Figure 1. *On a reach or in moderate wind, the wake is straight aft indicating no leeway. When sailing to weather in stronger winds leeway sets in and the wake appears to shift to windward as the boat slips to leeward. Schematic drawing adopted from the Starpath Online course on Inland and Coastal Navigation (www.starpath.com/courses). In the golden age of sailing when sailing ships slipped very much more than today it was common advice to new helmsmen to "Keep your wake right astern."*

To read one treatment of this from that era see Lecky's, Wrinkles in Practical Navigation, page 664. We have made this link to get you a free copy of this great book: www.tinyurl.com/1918Lecky.

Wind Velocity (knots)

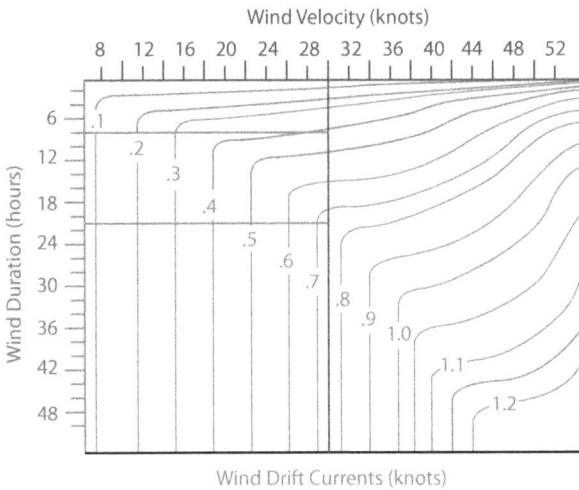

Figure 2. *This graph assumes a maximum wind drift current of about 2.5% of the wind speed when fully developed. Shown on the left are the times required to develop this current.*

The blue example marked shows a 30-knot wind producing a maximum of 0.75 knots, which would take some 19 hours to develop. When the wind has blown only 8 hours, the wind drift would be more like 0.4 knots.

Notice on the data that below about 30 kts, a required duration of half the wind speed is a good guess for maximum development, but at higher wind speeds it is more like hours = knots to get the water moving at max speed.

Adopted from the Starpath Weather Trainer Live software program.

we are discussing the reality of navigation, not a design parameter that may have a more complex interpretation.

Leeway can be discerned in your GPS derived data in special cases. For example, if the wind has just started to blow (so it has not had time to generate any surface current) and there are no other sources of current in the waterway, then when close hauled you will find your average COG to be some degrees to leeward of your average compass heading when steering a steady course on the wind, whereas your average SOG will match your average knotmeter speed. When this happens symmetrically on both tacks, you have a nice snapshot of your leeway. Sometimes you can actually see your wake bent to windward, which is the same effect. Yacht designers have developed underwater gimbaled vanes that measure the angle of motion through the water relative to the centerline for an accurate measurement of leeway vs wind speed and heeling angle.

With differential or WAAS enabled GPS, leeway shows up very nicely on units that directly compute current based on SOG and COG compared with accurate inputs of knotmeter speed and compass course. Going to weather in still water, you will have current on your windward beam regardless of your tack.

From a practical point of view, you can ignore leeway as soon as you fall off the wind. Above

some 45° apparent you can forget it unless you are still well heeled over or have other evidence that you might be slipping. Remember that leeway, unlike current, adds uncertainty only to your course direction, not your speed. In slack water, your knotmeter speed is your SOG even as you are slipping with leeway.

Leeway depends on wind speed. If your optimum wind speed is 10 knots true, then leeway increases going both up and down from there. In one sense, this is how optimum wind speeds are defined for sailing vessels. If it is, say 6° at optimum, then by the time you get to 20 knots it might be as high as 15°. In practice, however, it doesn't get much higher than this in normal operations because by then you start to fall off—except in some well designed race boats, it just doesn't pay to pound into the waves in very strong winds. And once you fall off, the slipping stops. Likewise at very low winds (a knot or two) you will also slip a lot, but again at some point you fall off and it goes away.

Leeway also depends on keel depth—the depth is much more important than the shape. Sailing a kayak, for example, just a paddle down in the water makes a world of difference. Likewise, to first approximation, a high tech racing keel and a full length cruising keel are about the same in this regard for a given depth. The high tech fin keel, however, can make up a lot by the actual lift it adds as water flows over it as wind does on airplane wings.

Leeway occurs in all waters, regardless of actual current flow. In strong winds, however, no water (ocean or lake) will stay still for long. When the wind blows steadily for half a day or longer it generates a surface current in any body of water. This new current must be added vectorially to the prevailing ocean or tidal current, or treated as a new issue in areas with no natural currents.

As a rule of thumb the strength of the wind drift is some 2.5% of the wind strength, directed some 20° to the right of the wind in higher northern latitudes and to the left of the wind in higher southern latitudes. In central latitudes the set is more in line with the wind. In Puget Sound or Juan de Fuca Strait and similar confined waterways where the land constrains the wind to flow along the waterway, wind drift here can be figured as essentially parallel to the waterways—with or against the tidal flow. In any waters, though, a 25-knot steady wind for a day or so will generate a current flowing downwind of some 0.6 knots.

In long heavy rains the wind driven current tends to be larger, since the brackish surface layer slips more easily over the denser salt water below. In extreme cases you might expect surface wind drift of over 3% in long, strong winds with much rain.

Helm bias is even more evasive in our navigation reckoning. Strong winds bring high seas (at least in the ocean) and with them the problem of steering over them. It is usually possible in these circumstances to detect a persistent course alteration at each wave. A common tendency going to weather is to fall off or get pushed off slightly at each wave. The only way to gauge this effect on the average course manually is to stand and watch the helm and compass for some time. Then make a guess at an average offset.

Or simply look at the track of a GPS plot of positions, which is what one would do in a normal situation—although it would still be difficult to pull out the helm bias from leeway and wind-driven current in some cases.

We are discussing DR here, however, and that means we are assuming we don't have these aids to look at. But it does bring up the important point that the best use of such wonderful nav aids is to use them to teach us about DR. In other words, when the waves start to build, confirm with the helmsman what course is being steered, and then watch the plot of positions to see what is being made good. There can of course be other influences (the subject at hand), but by noting what is being made good and then just standing there and watching the compass and the helm for a while, you can see what is taking place.

We are looking at going to weather here, which won't happen much in strong winds unless you are racing or trying to claw off a coast after getting in too close, but this same helm bias occurs going downwind as well. The bias sailing downwind tends to be to leeward (the right way) in big waves and fresh air, but in light air it might tend to be upwind in big waves as you try to keep the boat moving. So the summary is sailing to weather helm bias will most likely be to leeward, but sailing downwind it could be either way.

Also if you are navigating a race boat there can be numerous types of helm bias to watch out for, and they might be personality driven. Some drivers like to go fast regardless of what the course is supposed to be. Others might choose a more conservative course than called for to not risk a round up.

Here's an example to sum up these invisible problems. Going to weather across a 0.6 knot wind drift at 6 knots would set you off course some 5°, your leeway might be some 10°, and a helm bias account for another 5°. In this case the overall off-course set is about 20°. In the ocean, after 100 miles you would be some 30 to 40 miles off course to leeward if you did not figure these factors in your DR. Summarized another way, going to weather in a steady 20 to 25 kts of wind, will most likely cost you at least 20° of course made good.

When sailing to weather in strong winds, you will always be slipping down wind more than you might guess. While the GPS is still working, keep a record of what angles you actually tack through in big waves and strong winds—not compass headings, but the actual angle between the two track lines on the GPS plot. If you end up having to DR in these conditions without electronics, then it is usually a reasonable first guess to assume you did indeed cover the miles your log indicates, but then simply set the course made good some 20° to leeward.

When racing, there is an obvious advantage to tacking at the right time. If the electronics take a hike when you need them, these are the basics to fall back on. The compass headings alone won't help. In the above example, it would mean overstanding the windward mark by 20°.

Accuracy evaluation and statistical errors in DR are covered in detail in the book *Emergency Navigation*, because in an emergency without the aid of our accustomed instrumentation we are left with little but DR to go by. §

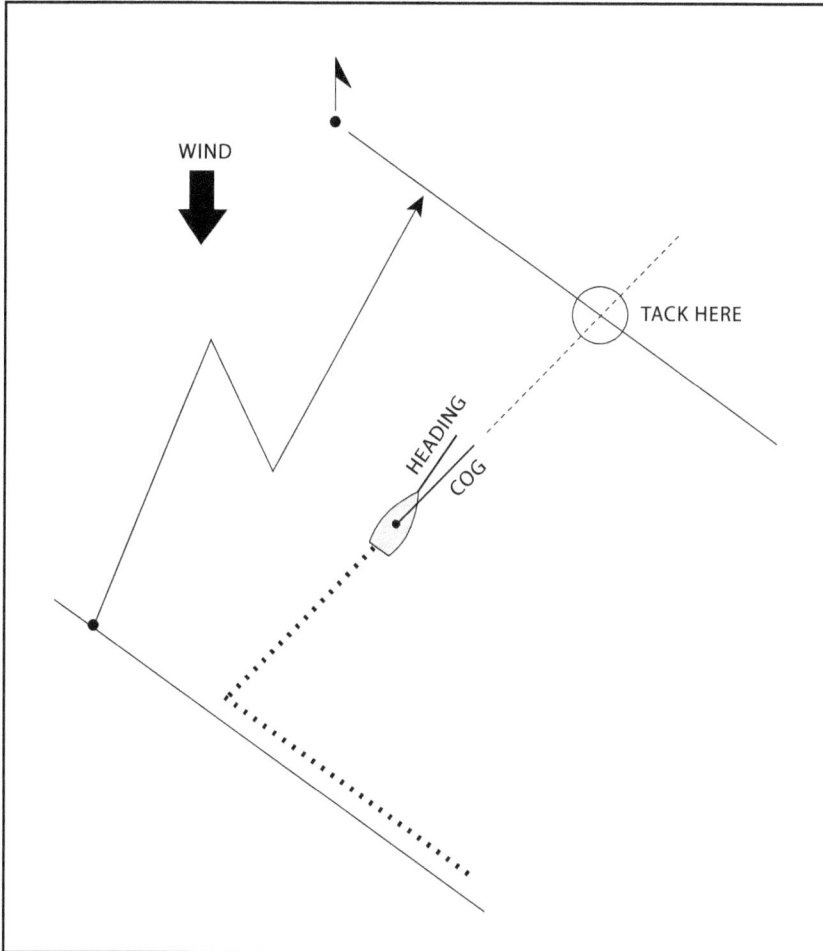

Figure 3. *How to use electronic charting display of your track to choose the time to tack when you are not making good the course you are steering. Here the boat is steering 045 on port tack in a northerly wind, but only making good 055. On a starboard tack, steering 315, you only make good 305. Once you have your actual tracks established on the chart on both tacks, you can then draw a range and bearing line parallel to the CMG of the final starboard tack, and move it to the windward mark. Then where that line crosses your last port tack line (projected from your COG), is when you tack to lay the mark. This would be the same maneuver to make if it were tidal current setting you off course rather than just wind.*

SEXTANT PILOTING

"The use of Hadley's quadrant [forerunner of the marine sextant], as an instrument to take altitudes at sea, is already so well established that it wants no further recommendation; but there are several other purposes, which though obvious enough, seem yet to be hardly sufficiently attended to. There is no instrument so well adapted to many kinds of piloting, either for exactness or convenience, and particularly the last; but the surveying of harbors, or such lands, as lie within sight of land, may oftentimes be performed by it, not only with vastly more ease, but also with a much greater degree of precision, than can be hoped for by any other means, as it is the only instrument in use, in which neither the exactness of the observations, nor the ease with which they may be taken are sensibly affected by the motion of the vessel; and hence a single observer in a boat, may easy determine the situation of any place he pleases, to twenty or thirty feet upon every three or four miles." —Rev. John Michell, BD, FRS, Philosophical Transactions of the Royal Society of London, 1765.

Rev. Michell was looking ahead farther than he knew. His observations remain equally valid and pertinent in 2013, which brings us to the subject at hand.

I am not sure what in the history of navigation led to the premature demise of these techniques. They dominated precision piloting throughout the 1800's and early 1900's, but then slowly fell from the standard textbooks. It could have been general improvements in time keeping, knotmeters, logs, compasses, and azimuth rings that led to better DR and bearing fixes in general, and certainly the onset of gyrocompasses and repeaters pushed the sextant deeper into the storage locker on inland waters. Electronic navigation then hid the key, and it was history, although well into the 80s one could periodically see a USCG vessel taking sextant piloting measurements when placing a buoy, even though Loran and other electronic aids were available. Sextant piloting remains the method of choice from the deck of any steel vessel, where magnetic bearing compasses are not dependable.

We are drawn back to sextant piloting in these modern days for several reasons.

First our beloved friend the GPS—the friend who told us the first one is free—is not on such stable footing as we might have taken for granted.

Check out the links to our current threats to GPS listed in the references. They include maritime vulnerabilities to GPS jamming and the anticipated influence of enhanced solar flares. Consider as well this question (#724) from the USCG database of license exam questions

Which statement concerning GPS is TRUE?

A. It cannot be used in all parts of the world.

B. There are 12 functioning GPS satellites at present.

C. It may be suspended without warning.

D. Two position lines are used to give a 2D fix.

The answer is C. If they had another question that read, "How do you know your GPS position is correct?" the right answer would be: You don't —unless you have some traditional geometric piloting technique to test it with.

At the end of last year when we lost the QuikSCAT satellite that provided the best weather data possible for all marine analysis, there was not a peep in the news, and there has not been any news since then. Now we have recently lost one of just two special satellites that form the basis of the Wide Area Augmentation System (WAAS). This is the differential GPS system whose satellites give us high precision GPS fixes and accurate derived functions such as speed and course over ground.

The WAAS satellites are always a boon to maritime navigation, but they are crucial to aviation use of GPS. There was no threat to safety because the failure came with ample warning, although 16 airports in NW Alaska are now without full use of their GPS and other users will experience delays because there are no backups—and still… not a peep in the public news. These would appear to be crucial technological failures, the implications of which are unclear. One cannot help but wonder if we are getting the full picture of our navigational situation from these agencies that are so strapped for cash because of such massive spending on war and bailouts.

You might say that when the Russian (Glonass) and European (Galileo) GPS systems are in full operation we will have back ups. Rough time estimates for these are maybe 1 year for Glonass —a system that was actually working once, fell into disrepair, and now is on the mend—and 4 years for Galileo; there is also a Chinese system called Compass further down the line. But you will need a new GPS unit to receive those signals (some are available now), but do we have reason to believe that competition in technology of this type might actually benefit the end user? Does having echarts from multiple nations make international electronic charting easier? The *Cosco Busan* hit the Bay Bridge in part because of a misunderstanding of symbols on a foreign echart. You can always paint one dongle red and another blue so they don't get mixed up! And what will the new GPS services cost? Some countries involved in the competing GPS technology actually copyright the harmonic constants God used when He made the tides go up and down, not to mention the shapes of their shorelines and the depths of their waters, also all copyrighted.

Looking ahead, there is every reason to believe that basic navigation skills, relying only upon our own wits and wisdom, will indeed have a place in our lives once again. To march foreword ignoring this is not prudent.

The other reason sextant piloting comes back to mind is the awareness that you do not need a "real" sextant to do it. That is, you do not need the type of sextant we think of when we hear the word—large, complex optical instrument, heavy, seemingly fragile, and certainly expensive. No. You can do it all and with amazing precision with a Davis Mark 3 plastic sextant that is actually quite durable in this application. The going price is under $60, but they often appear in sailor's swap meets, or on sale, for less.

Needless to say, you can do it with a high-quality metal sextant and whenever the angles are very small they are better done that way, but the bulk of the methods work fine with a simple plastic sextant, and some of the workhorse techniques are actually easier with a Mark 3 than with a full-sized metal sextant—mainly because the metal sextants are all much heavier.

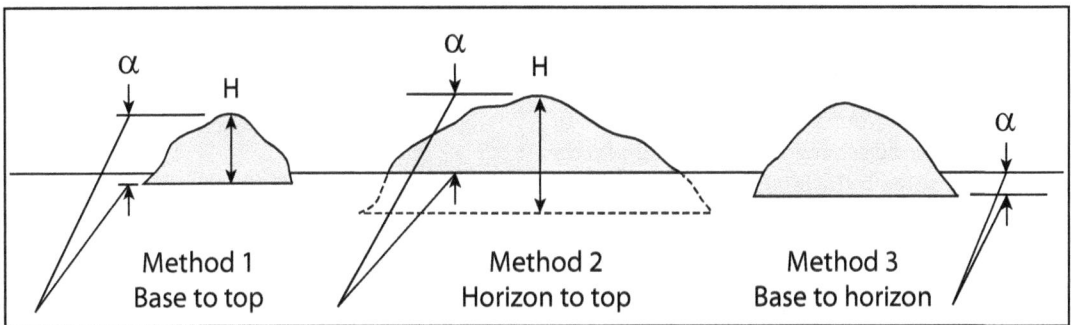

Figure 2. *In these sketches, a marks the angular height that is measured with a sextant and H is the charted elevation of the object. As an example for Method 1, H = 480 ft, a = 5.5°, HE = 9 ft, then the Bowditch calculator for Table 16 gives D = 0.82 nmi. The quick approximation gives 4.8/5.5 = 0.87 nmi. If H=900 ft and a = 1.2° with HE = 9 ft, we would get an approximate answer of 9/1.2 = 7.5 nmi, which is well beyond our horizon estimated at square-root (9) = 3 nmi, which implies we need to use* Bowditch *Table 15 calculator (Method 2) to get D = 6.7 nmi. If we can see an islet, or vessel, waterline notably below the horizon, we can figure the distance to it from the angular width of that gap using Method 3. For example, a = 0° 40' and HE = 9 ft, then from* Bowditch *Table 17 calculator we learn the object is D = 241 yards away. To avoid interpolation, the calculators are better than the printed tables. They will run in a smart phone.*

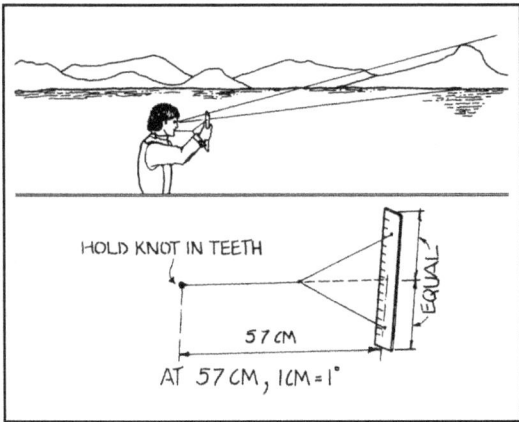

Figure 3. *Using a ruler as a makeshift sextant to measure the angular height of a hill. This is a modern version of ancient Arabic Kamal, used to navigate the East Coast of Africa following the monsoon winds up and down the coast. Illustration from* Emergency Navigation

Sextant piloting means finding out where you are from angles you measure with a sextant. Unlike sextant use in celestial navigation, we are now using all terrestrial targets and we must have a chart showing these targets for most applications.

There are two categories: vertical angles and horizontal angles. In both categories, you find a circle of position (COP) from the sextant sight, rather than a line of position (LOP) that you would find from a compass bearing or natural range. The intersection of two COPs or one COP and one LOP gives a position fix.

Vertical Angles

Your distance from a landmark (the radius of a COP) can be determined from vertical sextant angles three ways. If the landmark is shown on a chart, then you can use the result for chart navigation. If not, you are just finding your distance to it, wherever it is. For all vertical-angle methods you need to know your height of eye above the water (HE) at the location where you take the sight.

Method 1 (vertical, close). Measure the vertical angle between the top of an object whose height you know and the waterline at the object. Then with this measured angle (α) and the known height of the object (H) you can figure your distance to the object (D) from a set of tables or by direct computation. The table needed is *Bowditch* Table 16, which is available online as a pdf, along with a numerical calculator for the distance. See www.starpath.com/navpubs.

This is the most basic of the methods. We can use it to find distance to a peak, or distance to a vessel whose mast height we know. This is for closer targets whose waterlines must be above your horizon. You can get a good estimate of that distance in nautical miles from the square root of HE in feet. If your eye is 9 feet above the water, then the horizon cuts off your view at about 3.0 nmi. So if your answer turns out to be more than 3 miles (meaning you are not seeing the true base of the object because it is cut off by the curvature of the earth), then you need to use the analysis of Method 2. Same data, just different analysis.

Whenever Method 1 is valid, you can use an approximate solution for quick estimates. Use D(nmi) = H(ft)/100/α. When α (in degrees) is less than about 15° and HE is much less than H, then your distance to an object in nmi is just the height of the object in hundreds of feet divided by the angle in degrees. Then when we recall that 1 cm spans 1° at arm's length (which we call 57 cm), we can measure the angles with a small ruler for quick estimates of distance off of known objects. Without a ruler, we can use finger widths, which span about 1.5° each. These makeshift applications and how to "calibrate" your fingers are discussed in the book *Emergency Navigation*.

Figure 1. *A Davis Mark 3 plastic sextant is ideally suited for sextant piloting. Put it in Tupperware container with "$1000" written on the outside to remind you to care of it as if you paid that much for it, and it will serve you well for many years.*

Method 2 (vertical, far). When the base of the object is below your horizon, use Table 15 or its corresponding calculator. For target bases just over the horizon, this gives much the same answer as Method 1, but for the extreme cases when we just see the tip of a mountain on the horizon (α being a very small angle), it is crucial to use this formulation and be sure the sextant's Index Correction (IC) and your HE are accurate. This can be a valuable observation at the first sight of land after an ocean passage. It will be the first time you know if your GPS was right!

Method 3 (vertical, dip). This measurement can be a trick play for racing sailors who want to know how far off a competitor is and they do not have radar. It will work whenever you can see a horizon beyond and above the target vessel. Then use a sextant to measure how far the waterline of the vessel (or islet) is below the horizon, and use Table 17 (or corresponding calculator) to find distance off. Again, for this one, which will have very small angles, you need an accurate IC and HE, and careful measurements.

Threats to GPS

GPS jamming see gpsworld.com

Effects of solar flares see avweb.com

Loss of WAAS satellite see avweb.com

WAAS and aviation see faa.gov

A report at the time concluded with "A follow-up notification will be posted to this page once the full impact of the technical difficulties has been assessed. In the meantime, this information is being provided as a courtesy to our WAAS users." Some scientists believed the loss was due to enhanced solar activity.

Horizontal Angles

Distance-off measurements by sextant provide a means of finding a position fix from a single landmark and in that sense contribute to the step from the "ordinary knowledge of seaman" to that of a navigator. Most basic fixes we learn require two identifiable landmarks, such as two crossed compass bearings or two (transit) ranges, or maybe a range and a depth contour. The step to finding position from a single body, such as doing a running fix from the only light showing through in the fog, is a key one to becoming a versatile navigator, and distance off by sextant adds another method to this category. The distance from a peak and the compass bearing to that same peak provides a position fix from just one landmark.

Now we come to the real claim-to-fame of sextant piloting by turning the sextant sideways and measuring the horizontal angles between known landmarks on the horizon. From this we can find our position to remarkable accuracy—accurate enough to check the GPS in many circumstances. This procedure has attracted navigators and mathematicians since the very invention of the sextant in the mid 1700s. The procedure can be done with the simplest of plastic sextants or with your best ocean going instrument.

The horizontal angle between two landmarks on the horizon determines a unique circle of position on the chart (COP) that you must be located upon in order to observe that angle. As it is with a line of position (LOP) that you might get from a compass bearing to a lighthouse, you know you are on that circle, but you don't know where on the circle.

The procedure is to hold the sextant sideways, parallel to the ground, and measure the angle AB between two objects, A and B. For analogy to the vertical sights, one object serves as the horizon for the other. It is like taking a compass bearing to each of them and then subtracting to get the angle between them, only now we do this very accurately. We are very lucky to get compass bearings accurate to ±2°, but with a sextant we can easily measure the angle to within ±0.02° (1.2′)—and with care, much better than that.

The crux of this method is how you plot that unique COP on the chart knowing the location of the two objects and the angle between them. There are several methods. The simplest, mentioned mostly to illustrate the principle, is use the compass rose to fold a piece of paper to the angle measured, then slide it around on the chart keeping one side on each object, marking a point at the apex the triangle every so often. In doing so, you see clearly the principle behind the method, but this is not a very tidy solution. There is a special plotting tool, called a three-arm protractors (or station pointer), that makes this easier and more accurate—for this application, you only use two of the arms.

Without a three-arm protractor, you can plot the COP from a purely graphical solution as shown in the illustration, or use the compromise shown which combines a quick computation with a simple plot. One of these three methods is required to draw the COP on the chart—assuming you actually want the COP on the chart.

In a moment we look at reasons for drawing a COP on the chart, but if your goal is to get an actual fix, not just a COP, then you do not have to plot anything if you have the 3-arm protractor. Just take one more sight and then use a three-arm protractor for a quick and accurate fix, without drawing any lines at all. The process is illustrated in the figure using 3 landmarks, A, B, and C, with angles A to B and B to C.

This type of fix can be used to check the GPS, or when anchored in a steep sided bay with no GPS, this is ideal for checking to see if you are dragging anchor.

It is a seemingly simple process, but there are subtleties involved. The engaging issue is that some configurations of landmarks offer better accuracy than others, and the challenge has been to make the best set of guidelines for the navigator to use in choosing the optimum targets. Lecky devoted a full chapter of 30 pages to this topic and the associated use of a station pointer. One of the last editions of *Bowditch* that included guidelines for a good 3-body fix was the 1938 edition, which gives these criteria:

(a) When the center object of the three lies between the observer and a line joining the other two, or lies nearer than either of the other two

(b) When the sum of the right and left angles is equal to or greater than 180°

(c) When two of the objects are in range, or nearly so, and the angle to the third is not less than 30°

(d) When the three objects are in the same straight line

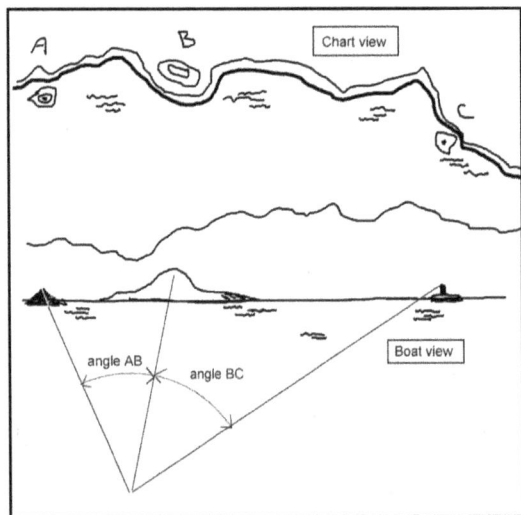

Figure 4. *Schematic view of three potential targets for a horizontal sextant angle fix, as they might appear from the boat and on a chart.*

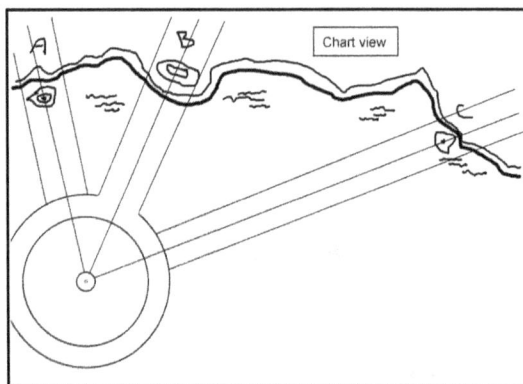

Figure 5. *Using a three-arm protractor to plot a horizontal sextant angle position fix. Set left arm to angle AB and set right arm to angle BC, then holding the angles fixed, slide the protractor around the chart till each arm crosses through its target and your position is in the center of the protractor which includes a small hole for a pencil mark. Without a three-arm protractor, the fix can be found graphically by plotting both circles of position.*

A Way to Practice

The best approach is to just do it. And here is a wonderful way to practice right from home without having to go to the boat. Look around your neighborhood for three prominent landmarks (A,B,C) some distance off that span some reasonable spread of the horizon (see guidelines above). Then check that you can identify these target objects on the Google Earth image of your location. You can use edges of distant buildings or even telephone poles a block or two away. The image view might help you locate good targets. Now use a sextant to measure the angles A to B and B to C. Print the image from Google Earth as large as you can that shows all objects and where you were standing. This is your "chart."

Then use the methods outlined above to find out where you were when you took the sights. This is an easy way to learn the nuances and beauties of the method very quickly. The references given go into details of the process and analysis. It is an engaging navigation sport—and a good way to survey your local bay if you care to. We have an uncharted rock just barely awash in our local bay that kayakers and stand up paddlers hit periodically at near-zero tide. With these techniques we could locate it precisely and put it on local charts till we have time to permanently mark it with a float.

Danger Circles

You can use the COP itself to enhance a bearing fix by plotting the two compass bearings to A and B and then measure the angle A to B to get a COP. Chose your best fix as the point on the COP closest to the intersection of the two bearing lines. This is analogous to a standard technique of radar navigation using tangent bearings and a range.

Another application is to use a COP as a danger circle to keep you away from known dangers

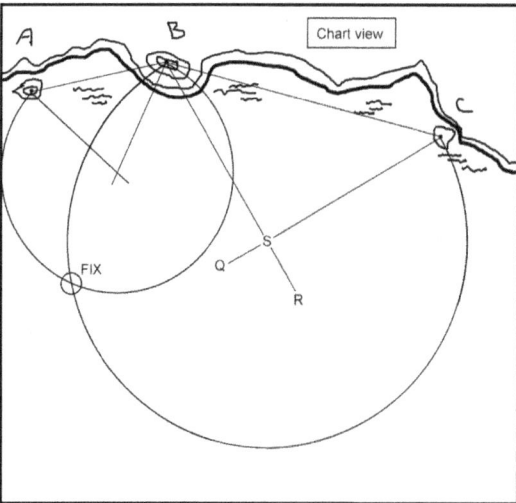

Figure 6. *Graphic solution to the three-body problem. There are numerous solutions. This is the easiest if we do not include numeric computations in the process.*

Plot procedure:
1, Draw line B-C
2. Construct angle CBR = 90°- angle BC
3. Construct Angle BCQ = 90°- angle BC
4. From intersection S, draw circle with radius SC
5. Vessel is on that circle

Do the same with measured angle AB.
Fix is the intersection of those two circles.

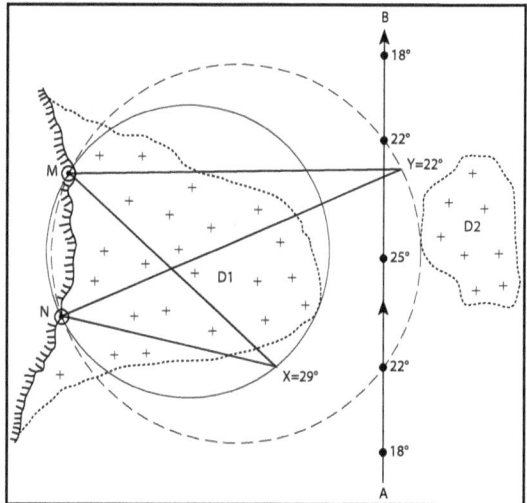

Figure 7. *Using the horizontal sextant angle between two landmarks, M and N, to guide you between two underwater hazards, D1 and D2, along course A to B. As you proceed from A the angle will begin to drop. Everywhere on the solid circle the angle MN=29°; everywhere on the dashed circle, MN=22°. Once you cross over the MN=22° COP you want to be sure that the MN angle stays larger than 22 and smaller than 29. The peak will be at about 25. With someone to help, one person keeps M and N in view in the sextant at all times, calling out the angles, while another person steers. Picture adapted from a 1962 Bowditch.*

that you must pass in the presence of currents that could set you toward them. Once you find the sextant angle that marks your safe bearing, you monitor that angle as you pass and do not let yourself get set to a place where the angle reads larger than the danger angle. It is exactly analogous to using a danger bearing monitored by bearing compass, which is a common solution to this problem for those without radar. With radar, the variable range marker is usually the simplest and quickest solution to staying a fixed distance off a good radar target. The well prepared navigator must have a deep bag of tricks to cover the varying circumstances that might occur, such as dangers off of a low flat beach that is not a good radar target.

The procedure is to find the sextant angle that makes a COP that encompasses the danger and then keep the sextant angle smaller (or larger) than that as you pass. As shown in the illustra-tions, this takes some plotting ahead of time, so this method is best done in preparation for a known hazard you must pass in the future. You can pre-draw several such COP segments on the chart to monitor your progress. In the example shown you would be hard pressed to solve that problem with danger bearings. You might want to use this method to back up your GPS anyway if you had to make this passage—we do still have the basic rule of good navigation that you should not rely on one aid alone if the matter is crucial.

For those involved in GPS caching games, you should be able to stash a prize in a location relative to local landmarks in view using sextant piloting more accurately than you can with a GPS, which will often have uncertainties of ±50 ft or more. To convince yourself, find a place in your backyard this way, then take a large step to the left and do it again. GPS is not even a close competitor to the sextant in this type of navigation! §

More Practice

Here is an example of the types of problems 19th century navigation students solved routinely using the methods presented here. From the Twelfth Edition of Noire, 1839. The description of the lighthouse locations lets us plot them on a blank paper to make a chart at any scale we choose.

From Winterton Lighthouse to Hasborough High Lighthouse the bearing and distances are N. 41° 40' W at 8.54 miles, and from the latter to Cromer Lighthouse N 51° 6'W at 9.64 miles. From our vessel, the angle between Winterton and Hasborough High Lighthouses, measured by sextant, was 28° 35', and between the latter and Cromer Lighthouse 59° 8'. Find the bearings and distances from the vessel to each of the three lighthouses. Note that N41° 40'W = 318.3T, etc. Cromer is still there; Winterton is a private home; and Hasborough may be Happisburgh. Actual 1800's locations are likely different because much of the Norfolk coastline has been eroded since the 1600s when these lights were first established.

Answers:

To Comer: S 76° 7'W at 10.42 miles

To Hasborough High: S 16° 59'W at 8.945 miles (I get 9.1, but agree with the others)

To Winterton: S 11° 36'E at 15.24 miles

References

Wrinkles in Practical Navigation, S.T.S. Lecky (Geo Philip & Sons, 22nd ed., 1947). Online in full in various editions from 1881.

A Complete Epitome of Practical Navigation, J.W. Norie (J. W. Norie & Co., 12th ed. 1839). Norie's long series of editions have been described as the British Bowditch. Online in full in various editions from 1835.

Inland and Coastal Navigation, David Burch (Starpath Publications, 2009). See especially section 12.30 by mathematician Dr. John Hocking on horizontal sextant angles.

Emergency Navigation, David Burch (McGraw Hill, 2nd ed., 2009)

Radar for Mariners, David Burch (McGraw Hill, 2005)

How to Use Plastic and Metal Sextants, David Burch (Starpath Publications, October, 2010). A new, enhanced edition of How to Use Plastic Sextants, with an extended section on sextant piloting.

www.starpath.com/navpubs has links to early navigation texts and other nav resources

www.ion.org/museum has details of a station pointer at the Institute of Navigation's Virtual Museum. See under Marine/Map Plotting tools

TRAFFIC IN THE FOG

Picture this. You are cruising through a thick fog, a hundred miles from land, and out of the grey silence you suddenly hear a loud prolonged blast of a fog horn. It sounds close, and it seems to be from somewhere on the port bow. What do you do? We could end up in the same circumstance within a mile from land in some cases.

That is, in a nutshell, the subject at hand. And as we will see, we need to know more about the situation before we can answer this question, and it will help to review the background. The key point is whether or not we have radar available. If we did, we were presumably using it for some time leading up to this moment. In any event, we are going to be careful. In this article we will look at the background common to both encounters and cover without radar first. Next month we address the use of radar.

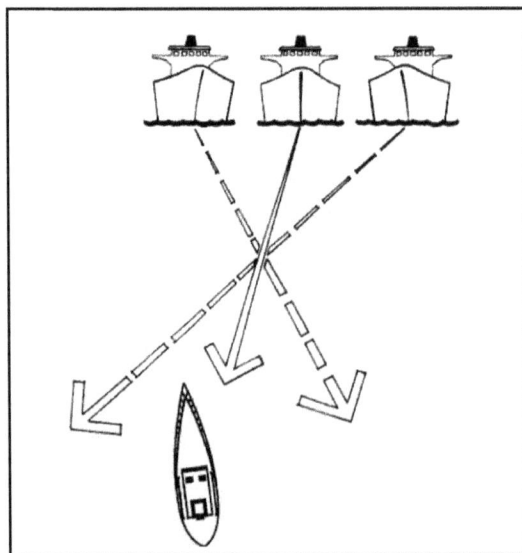

Figure 1. *Judging relative course lines at close quarters by watching the ship's bow relative to its superstructure. This observation is clearly made from within an extreme situation that we would want to avoid getting into.*

There are distinctly different rules on how vessels are supposed to interact with each other in clear weather (day or night), as opposed to how they interact in restricted visibility, when they cannot see each other visually. The laws and guidelines are presented in the Navigation Rules. A fundamental tenet in clear weather is that when two vessels approach each other in clear sight of each other, one has right of way over the other. The only exception in clear weather is when two vessels under power approach head to head, on reciprocal courses, in which case both must turn right. The Rules don't say who goes first or why, because it does not matter. Both must turn.

Also fundamental to the Rules—in all conditions of visibility—are the concepts of *risk of collision* and *close quarters*, neither of which is defined explicitly in the Rules themselves. A working definition of close quarters, which can withstand the scrutiny of the courts, is to think of it as that space around you that is required for your own maneuver to avoid a collision (in the circumstances at hand), regardless of what the other vessel might do, suddenly and unexpectedly. This is your space; as long as you have this space you are safe. If you anticipate a vessel entering this space with any doubt at all that it will pass safely, then the Rules give you the right and indeed obligation to maneuver to get back your space, regardless of what other Rules might be in effect at the time. The extent and shape of the close-quarters space depends on the circumstance. Passing another vessel at slow speed in a narrow cut it could be a matter of yards; interacting with full speed ships in the ocean, it is more often a matter of miles.

In the fog, an understanding of the concepts of collision risk and close quarters become even more crucial because the very nature of the Rules change when you are interacting with vessels you can't see visually—that is, with vessels you hear or detect by radar alone. You must then rely more often and more heavily on your personal definition of these key concepts. In the fog, there is no stand-on vessel and no give-way vessel.

No one (sail, power, or paddle) has right of way in the fog. All vessels are given the same instructions. They appear in Rule 19, Conduct of Vessels in Restricted Visibility. This is the key rule, although fundamental Rules 5 to 8 on Proper Look-out, Safe Speed, Risk of Collision, and Action to Avoid Collision still apply, as they are specified as valid in all conditions of visibility.

How you comply with Rule 19 depends on whether or not you have radar on board and working. Rule 7(a), by the way, says that if you have radar you must use it, and Rule 7(c) says, specifically, that you should use it properly, which implies a basic understanding of how to use radar to detect risk of collision and related observations, such as how to tell if a target moving toward you on the radar screen is one you are overtaking or one that is headed toward you.

Radar is undoubtedly the most important electronic aid to collision avoidance and perhaps to navigation in general, but there is a clear obligation to learn its use that follows it onto the boat. It is a small price to pay, however, for the safety and efficiency it affords. The book *Radar for Mariners* and the PC radar simulator "Starpath Radar Trainer" are good ways to master these skills. We cover use of radar in collision avoidance next month.

Without Radar

When traveling in the fog without radar, you can only know of approaching traffic from their fog signals (one prolonged blast every 2 minutes for a ship making way), or by hearing their engines. In principle you could also hear a ship calling an "unidentified vessel" on your VHF, but that is not you detecting them. (If such radio communications do occur be certain that all vessels are properly identified. I have seen a case where a ship called one sailboat and another answered and started to discuss the interaction, and it took precious long time to sort this out.)

According to Rule 19 (e), if we hear a fog signal "apparently forward of the beam" we are instructed to slow to the minimum speed needed to hold course, and if necessary take all way off, and in any event navigate with extreme caution.

Clearly, though, in a small vessel which is a poor radar target, we must consider any noise we hear as a warning for extreme caution.

Note there are no instructions for altering course in these circumstances, nor any justification for it. Turning away from a fog signal is not helpful, and would just confuse anyone watching you on radar. "Extreme caution," clearly suggests using the VHF radio immediately to try to reach the signaling vessel, and here an accurate GPS position could be very helpful. The prudence of a handheld VHF at the wheel in such conditions is obvious.

There is not much else you can do, other than repeat your own fog signal (one prolonged and two shorts for a vessel under sail) aimed in the apparent direction you heard from. It is unlikely this would be heard from a ship, unless they were moving slowly with a bow watch, but it could be heard from smaller vessels—or you could actually make one that could be heard from a car horn operated on your 12V system. Then you wait, and listen, and be ready to maneuver immediately. Drifting along in the fog in an area of known traffic without wind and without your engine on and no way for a ready maneuver is prohibited in 19(b).

One advantage a sail boat has in light air in the fog is you can hear very well. Ship signals are often on timers so they will sound precisely every two minutes, or whatever smaller interval they are using. Check your watch to know when to listen for the next one. Keep in mind that the apparent distance off of sounds is not very reliable in the fog, and the directions to them are not much better, but the directions can in some cases be useful—else why would they word the Rules to include that observation. A good radar reflector is a must. Ask a passing vessel to check your radar echo some time in clear weather.

In the most frightening situation, when the signal we hear from any direction is obviously very close, we can anticipate being in extremis, meaning that at this point collision avoidance is going to be up to our maneuver alone. We should slow to bare steerage as quickly as possible and turn toward the apparent direction of the danger we hear. A head-on approach presents a smaller target and gives us the best chance for a quick maneuver to either side, and if we should collide

Figure 2. *A true story, told to us at a boat show, except the captain's actual thought was phrased rather differently... and someone also needs a copy of the* Navigation Rules

near head to head, we have a better chance of getting pushed aside rather than smashed.

Clearly if much travel must be made in the fog in the presence of traffic, radar is definitely called for. One does not have to go through many encounters like this to agree. I get nervous just writing about it. And raw fatalism has no role in prudent seamanship. The problem we face when unprepared with our own equipment is the misjudgment too often made by ship captains that the sophistication of their own radar justifies high speed in the fog. The courts never agree, but that is beside the point.

When we put ourselves in position to hear the Charon call of a fog signal bearing down on us from a mile or so off in an uncertain direction, giving us 3 or 4 minutes to get our lives in order, when we could have known a half an hour ago that something was coming, and not long after that where it was going, then we have pumped more adrenaline into our sailing than need be—and have probably mis-allocated our equipment budget.

With Radar

Last month we discussed issues of navigating near traffic in the fog without radar. This month we bring the anxiety level down a great deal and discuss the use radar. Radar makes such interactions much safer, but we must learn how to use it to take advantage of the safety it offers, which includes understanding the Rules that govern it use. There are indeed such things as "radar assisted collisions."

The concept of close quarters discussed earlier is still crucial—maybe even more so. A practical way to think of close quarters is to consider it the room around you that you need to maneuver on your own to prevent a collision, regardless of what an approaching vessel might do, suddenly and unexpectedly. As long as you do not allow another vessel into that space, you should be safe. The Navigation Rules gives you the right, and even obligation, to maneuver to protect that space, regardless of what other rules may also apply.

It is also the same rule that covers both cases, with and without radar, namely Rule 19—Conduct of Vessels in Restricted Visibility. With radar on board, the instructions appear in Part (d). Look carefully to what the rule says, without assuming anything it does not say—that is a good guide to understanding all of the Nav Rules, but it is especially important for this one.

Whenever a radar target first appears on the radar screen, no matter where it is located on the screen, there is an immediate call to action:

Step (1). Watch the target to see if a risk of collision or a close-quarters situation is developing. We do this by marking it on the radar screen with pen, or use the electronic bearing line (EBL) and variable range marker (VRM). A vis-à-vis overhead projector marker is a good choice for on the screen marks. Or record the target's range, bearing, and time on the border of a chart. If you have it, turn on the "wake" or "trail" option to record on the screen the motion of the target.

In the language of Rule 7(b), use some "systematic observation." Any fast ship in open water that is headed toward a passing of within 2 or 3 miles of you, is headed toward a potential risk of collision. And if you have been watching a target at all on a small boat radar from some 10 or so miles off, then it is definitely a ship—or a drilling platform. Also recall from Rule 7(b) that you will be checking the long ranges as well as the close ones when doing your radar watch, so you will spot it early.

The range of acceptable passing distance will be up to you. I have sailed on race boats where less than a mile in the fog in strong wind was tolerated by a full, highly trained crew who knew the boat well, and I have sailed with very experienced top-notch ocean sailing instructors used to sailing short handed or with less experienced crew on boats they might not know as well who

do not want to come within 5 miles of a ship at night, even in clear weather, let alone in the fog. The more common choice is likely between these two examples.

Step (2). If collision risk or close quarters is developing, "take avoiding action in ample time." Note the big difference here between the instructions of this rule and other rules covering interactions of vessels in sight of each other. Section II rules (in sight of one another) tell us what to do when already within the risk of collision or close quarters in order to avoid a collision. Here (in Section III rules for restricted visibility) we are instructed to avoid the risk itself. "In ample time" means maneuver before the risk of collision or close quarters occurs. It is a stronger rule, calling for earlier action than when in a corresponding encounter in clear weather.

The rule applies to both vessels. If I see the target getting close to me on my radar, then that target sees me getting close to him on his radar. There is no holding course and speed by anyone during an interaction in the fog, even if you are being overtaken. Your job—the job of both vessels observing each other on radar—is to maneuver so that you do not get into a situation where there is risk of collision. In other words, we are to stay farther apart than when passing in clear weather and the burden of seeing to this separation lies on both vessels, not on just one as in the case of clear weather.

Step (3). If you alter course as part of your maneuver—which is the most common reaction, but not necessarily the best in all circumstances—the direction you turn depends on where the target is on the radar screen. For targets approaching from forward of your beam (on either side), you turn right. For targets approaching on the beam or aft of the beam, you turn away from the target. In other words, we are instructed to turn right for

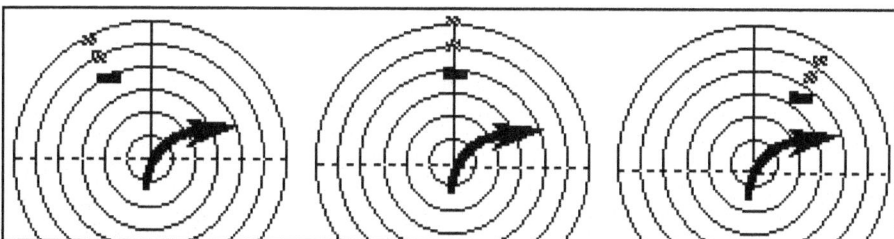

Figure 3. *Forward of the beam turn right...*

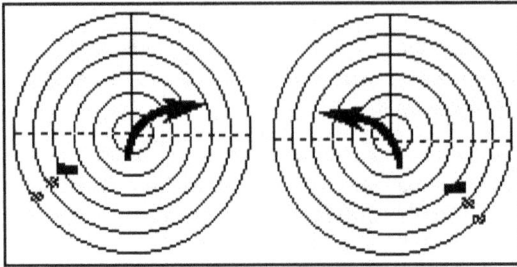

Figure 4. ...Aft turn away

all approaching vessels except those on the quadrant of the starboard quarter. Or for an easier way to remember it:

Forward of the beam turn right,

aft of the beam turn away.

The only situation where it might not be clear immediately what direction to turn is when a target is approaching on the starboard beam when it is not clear if he is slightly forward or slightly aft of right on the beam. In this case you might want to consider slowing down rather than turning. In any event, the instructions go on:

Step (4). If for any reason you cannot avoid a close quarters situation with a vessel forward of your beam, then you must slow down to bare steerageway, and if necessary take all way off and navigate with extreme caution—the same as if you had heard a fog signal forward of the beam without radar.

It is, however, very unlikely that you would get into this situation with radar. In almost all of such cases, if you are on a collision course with a vessel according to the radar and you are still moving, then stopping alone will pull his radar track "up-screen" enough to remove the immediate risk and give you time to further evaluate the situation. More generally, if the target is already going to pass forward of you, then slowing will open up the passing distance. It pays to remember that the other vessel may not be watching its radar at all, nor even have one.

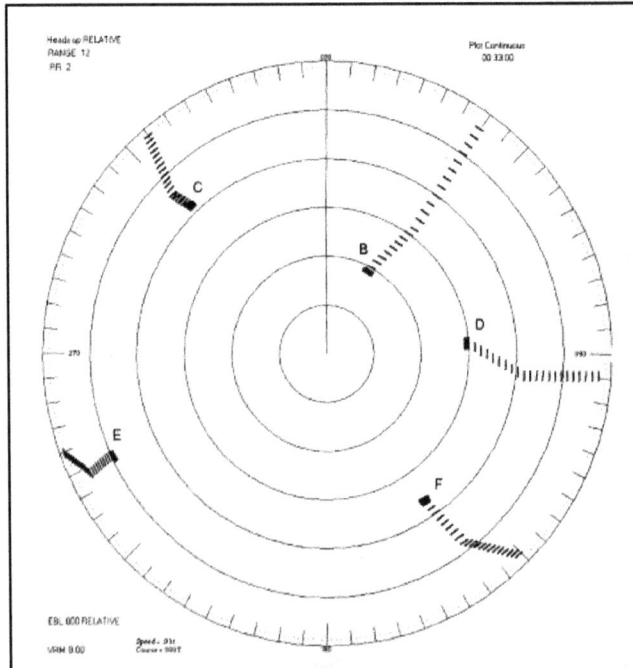

Figure 5. *When we slow or stop, all target vessel trails turn upscreen, in any radar display mode. This picture, captured from the Radar Trainer simulator, shows the effect for 5 targets approaching from different quadrants. Our original speed was 6 kts and our heading was 000, and then we stopped. The stop took place at plot clock reading 17:00, where the kinks in the trails are located, then the data accumulated for another 16 minutes to plot clock reading 33:00. Note that in all cases the directions of relative motion (DRMs) turned up-screen when we stopped. In this example, the 2 targets E and F that were safely passing astern when we were moving are now on converging courses.*

The effect of your speed changes on the radar target trails you observe may sound complicated in this radar context of relative motion, but in clear weather without radar it is completely obvious. You see a crossing vessel coming toward you on a collision course, so you stop and he passes in front of you!

Rule 19 is explicit in all circumstances on what turns should be made when choosing to turn—although slowing down for targets that are already going to pass in front of you may be the better call. There are only two optional maneuvers that might come to play involving overtaking from dead astern. When you are certain the target approaching from forward of the beam is one you are overtaking, then you have the option to pass on either side, which could involve a turn to the left to open the distance. Once he sees what side you are on (as a target approaching from aft of his beam), he should move the other way to open the passing distance farther. A vessel would show up on the radar screen as one you are overtaking if his radar target is moving down your screen at a relative speed distinctly slower than your own speed. A radio contact would clarify this.

The other option also occurs in overtaking, when a target approaches overtaking you from exactly astern, in which case you could turn either way if you think it is getting too close on this course. He is overtaking you, so he has the option to go either side, although, it is clearly not good seamanship on his part to run up the stern of a vessel he is watching on the radar, assuming he is watching you on radar. Your 90° turn at some point should solve the problem.

In all such maneuvers, Rule 8(b) applies: maneuvers should be large enough to be readily apparent on the other's radar—which calls for big turns, 60° or more. And so does Rule 7(c): assumptions about risk of collision should not be made on the basis of scanty radar information—often meaning when the target is too far away, or when your course is varying so much that you can't establish a clear radar-screen trace of the approaching target. If you can't figure out what is going on while you are moving, then you must slow down or stop to figure it out, as stated in Rule 8(e). As mentioned earlier, Rules 5 to 8 all apply in the fog as well as clear weather and are worth reviewing. These, along with Rule 19, in their official wording, should be referred to for study. Paraphrasing the rules as done here is always a risky business.

Once a vessel emerges from the fog and you can see each other visually, the operative rules revert back to the standard steering and sailing rules, wherein one vessel will be obligated to stay clear of the other. Consequently, it pays to estimate the range of visibility and, from the present range and bearing of radar targets, estimate when and at what bearing they should emerge from the fog, thinking ahead on what your response will be at that time. Near Vessel Traffic Service lanes, where the services include regularly scheduled or periodic broadcasts of ship locations, it is crucial to monitor these broadcasts, plot the ship positions, and figure the ETA of your passing.

The author's book *Radar for Mariners* explains these points further with suggested specific maneuvers based on target location and distance off. The Starpath Radar Trainer PC radar simulator is an effective and realistic way to practice these matters from the kitchen table; both are available from www.starpath.com, which also offers a complete online course on marine radar. §

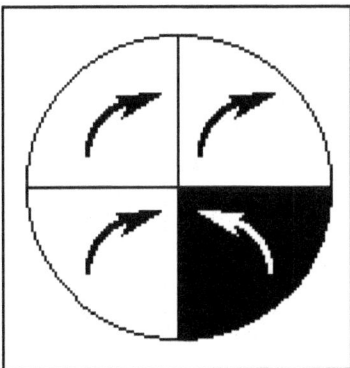

Figure 6. *Summary*

Selected Navigation Rules about Radar*

From Section I—Conduct of Vessels in Any Condition of Visibility

Rule 7

(b) Proper use shall be made of radar equipment if fitted and operational, including long-range scanning to obtain early warning of risk of collision and radar plotting or equivalent systematic observation of detected objects.

(c) Assumptions shall not be made on the basis of scanty information, especially scanty radar information.

Rule 8

(b) Any alteration of course and/or speed to avoid collision shall, if the circumstances of the case admit, be large enough to be readily apparent to another vessel observing visually or by radar; a succession of small alterations of course and/or speed should be avoided.

(e) If necessary to avoid collision or allow more time to assess the situation, a vessel shall slacken her speed or take all way off by stopping or reversing her means of propulsion.

From Section III—Conduct of Vessels in Restricted Visibility

Rule 19

(d) A vessel which detects by radar alone the presence of another vessel shall determine if a close-quarters situation is developing and/or risk of collision exists. If so, she shall take avoiding action in ample time, provided that when such action consists of an alteration of course, so far as possible the following shall be avoided:

(i) an alteration of course to port for a vessel forward of the beam, other than for a vessel being overtaken;

(ii) an alteration of course toward a vessel abeam or abaft the beam.

(e) … every vessel which… cannot avoid a close-quarters situation with another vessel forward of her beam, shall reduce her speed to the minimum at which she can be kept on her course. She shall if necessary take all her way off and in any event navigate with extreme caution until danger of collision is over.

* Please refer to the full wording of the full set of the Navigation Rules. Samples presented out of context like this do not convey the full intention and import of the Rules. The Rules are available online at www.starpath.com/navpubs.

OCEAN &
CELESTIAL
NAVIGATION

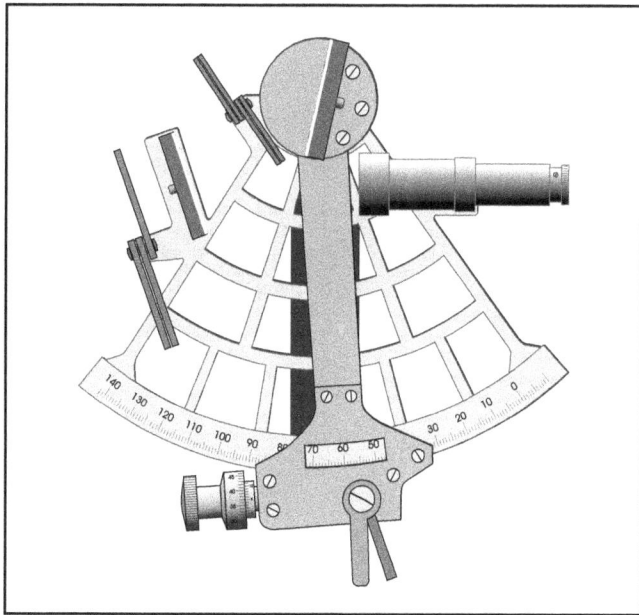

THE OCEAN-GOING NAV STATION

Every practicing navigator has an ideal nav station in mind—the place of work, its location, its layout, its tools. The ideal usually comes about the hard way, by ruling out, piece by piece, systems, locations, and things that don't work well. Somehow things that don't work make a bigger impression than things that do. As it is with learning any aspect of sailing, the best way to find your own ideal is to sail and navigate on different boats. At least with navigation, it won't take too long to find out what works well for you.

Here I will share some of my ideals and try to point out ones that I think most navigators would agree on as opposed to ones that are just my preference. For example, I prefer to sit facing forward because it is easier for me to think through course changes, tacking angles, wind shifts, and so on when I am facing the way I am going. But this is just a preference. Chart table work in rough seas is not much different in any direction, if the seat is well designed, and I suspect that if I did it always one way, regardless of what way it was, I would also learn to think more easily in that orientation.

First the seat. A comfortable seat is important because you sit a lot when navigating. Or, rather, you should sit if you can. It's hard to think standing up, as the old saying goes—especially if your back aches, and even the strongest backs ache leaning over a chart table for an hour or so. Luckily it's a rare stand-up chart table that won't accommodate some form of seat. With some ingenuity you can design one that can be removed when not in use to free up the space they were intended to provide in the first place.

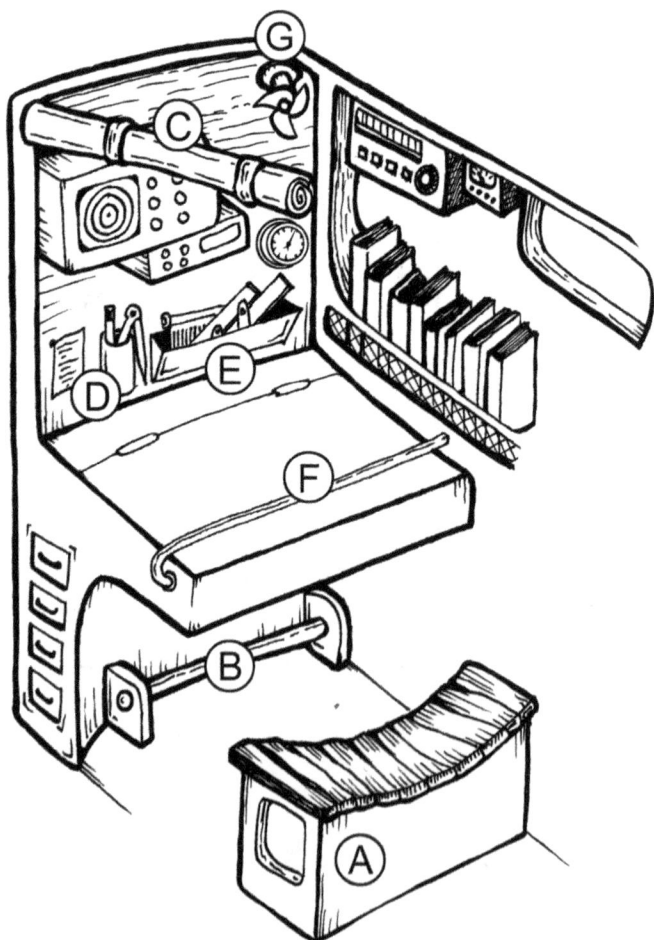

Figure 1. *An ocean going nav station. A. Curved seat helps you stay vertical when heeled. B. Footrest so knees can be wedged up under the table to hold you in place in the waves. C. Spray Curtain to keep light in at night, and water out always. Some boats use two; one clear for daylight, one opaque for night. D. Pencil holder, also holds dividers and flashlight. E. Holder for parallel rulers and plotters. F. Bungee to hold chart table lid down. It also holds charts and books in place when underway. G. Fan for navigator's comfort!*

One kind of chart table seat I found very comfortable was cut on an arc so that (when facing forward) you are always sitting straight up-and-down regardless of the boat's heel. The seat is easy to make from 3/4-inch plywood front and back plates cut with an arc, and then the seat itself made from 1x2 slats screwed into the plywood.

The other end of the problem is the feet. For rough going you need some way to get wedged into the chart table seat. One nice solution is a small foot stool built into the sole under the table, or a ledge on the bulkhead in front of the table. These can be custom-made to your leg length so that when in use your legs are pinned against the bottom of the chart table, holding you in place with hands free. It's best to arrange the design so you can sit comfortably without using this brace since you only need it in rough conditions. Without a curved seat and foot brace, you may need to rig some form of seat belt system that will keep you in place when heeled over or when bouncing about for any reason.

The location of the nav station doesn't really matter much. They usually get placed next to the companionway, which is good since you can talk back and forth to the cockpit from there. But this is also a very wet place. So it pays to have a spray curtain built that hangs between you and the companionway. This serves two purposes. First it keeps your gear dry—or more precisely, limits the water on your charts to that which runs off of your own rain gear. Second it blocks out the light so your work at night does not interfere with the helmsman.

This last point is an important one. The navigator has to work at night, but it is equally important that no light at all get out to the cockpit. As you know, even the faintest light makes steering at night very difficult. Going fast in big waves on a dark night, the helmsman has very little for orientation and it can be dangerous to interfere with that. Often even stock steering compass lights are too bright in these cases. In short, it pays to think this through so you don't end up duct taping yourself into a cocoon.

As for the nav table lights themselves, I have never seen a specialized nav table light that found its way onto the ideal list. I refer here to the special ones of various designs intended to emit focused light or dim light or red light and so on. The famous, standard goose neck light, for example, is near useless since, goose neck or not, you can't see the whole chart with them. Lift the chart table lid, and you can't see anything. A different, more expensive type that comes close to solving the problem is mounted on a pivot and is detachable for hand use. It has variable intensity and a red light option. Perhaps two or three of these—one stored in a bag for hand use, since they can be difficult to get in and out of the pivot—might do the job, but it is not just a matter of buying one of these fancy lights and screwing it into wherever it seems to fit best. In any event, a 2xAAA flashlight (or equivalent) in the tools holder is a must for special use, such as reading dials, corners of a chart, etc.

For longer jobs, I prefer a fixed white light over the table and then cover the entire area someway. For short jobs, a hand held flashlight does the job well providing it has a permanent home near the table so you can always find it when you need it. Individuals will likely differ on this, but I find it difficult to see pencil lines in red light. Also the coloring on charts looks different in red light and takes some getting used to. Red light, by the way, has no special significance to protecting night vision. The main factor is intensity, and red lights are not bright, hence their value. A low level white light is just as good, and to me much preferable.

Seat and light are important, but not the most important. The single most important aid to navigation without doubt is a pencil holder (for pencils and dividers, and flashlight) and a holder for your parallel rulers or plotter that is within arm's reach in front of you, outside of the chart table. With these holders you can always find your tools when you need them and you always have a place to put them between uses. Otherwise they will get lost or broken. Without these holders, sometime in life you will want to draw a line, can't find a pencil, won't draw the line, and later regret it.

I used to strongly prefer thin-lead mechanical pencils, with the lead advance button down near the point, but this is obviously just a personal preference. Any pencil and a way to keep it sharp will do. A number 2 lead is traditionally considered optimum, with a number 1 lead claimed to be so soft that it smears, and number 3 too hard to see or erase. I prefer No.1 because it can be seen well on damp charts. Over the years, however, I have tended to migrate back to conventional No. 2 pencils, rather than mechanical—the lead change is probably related to sailing on larger boats that are drier! Again, though, the pencil plus sharpener system must be well tested. Sometimes we blame bad sharpening on the sharpener, when the problem is actually the pencil.

The space inside the chart table, under the lid, is essentially useless space to navigation. This may seem surprising, but check under the lids of a few chart tables to get the point—and you may get just that, the point of the dividers! The chart table is simply too convenient a place to store what ever has to be put down in a hurry. My standard advice is this: make an absolute rule that nothing at all gets put into the chart table. Then when it fills to overflowing, just forget about it. You will not be counting on that space.

Nevertheless, you still have a chart table lid to deal with, which must be secured for a 180° roll. We forgot that once during a pre-race inspection and was cited for it. But during the time the inspector checked the rest of the boat, we drilled a hole in the side of the chart table and one in the board beside it and stretched a bungee cord between them secured with figure eights inside to hold down the lid. To lift the lid, just pull the cord toward you; then put it back when you close the lid. This passed muster and off we went. However, this rule-beater solution actually turned out to be excellent. The cord not only does not get in the way, but serves very nicely for holding down charts and books while underway. I have sense used this same system on every ocean voyage with this type of standard chart table lid. You can remove the bungee in calm waters and the holes are barely noticeable. Or use bails underneath the table.

My favorite pencil holder is a short tube attached to a shelf or bulkhead. The tube from an empty toilet paper roll does the job in a pinch—duct taped over the bottom, with tissue stuffed inside to protect the bottom from divider points, then taped to the wall.

This elegant design has made it across oceans more than once. It holds pencils, pencil-type erasers, and dividers. As soon as engine keys, sunglasses, and various other things start appearing in it, remind people what the chart table is for. A tall square plastic fruit juice bottle is ideal for this type of pencil holder, and this is the type I have used for years, always having a few on hand and taking one onto each new boat. Some time ago in a magazine story about Whitbread Round the World race boats, they showed the nav station of one boat that had more than $75,000 worth of electronic nav gear, and right in the middle of this stuff was taped to the bulkhead this exact type of juice bottle used for a pencil holder. Needless to say, this vessel won my heart immediately.

If you carry a backup steering compass, the chart table top is a good place to store it, so it can be used for navigation reference at the table. When mounting it keep in mind what might be stored under it in drawers. Check it occasionally with the steering compass, and if they disagree start pulling drawers open to see if the compass needle moves. If it does, you found the villain.

Some hand-held bearing compasses can be mounted on or near the chart table and used for reference, but a dedicated, adjustable compass is the best bet. These days a digital fluxgate compass or an electronic repeater from a remote unit is the more likely option for a magnetic heading reference at the nav station. It is generally best to

Figure 2. *Russian course box seen on eBay.*

mount the hand-held bearing compass just inside the companionway so it can be reached from the cockpit without going below. Again, it will be used more often if it is easy to get to. Needless to say, the compass at the nav station has to be adjusted and its calibration monitored.

Besides the compass, it is very convenient to have electronic readouts at the nav station for all navigation instruments. This makes logbook entries easier for everyone and makes the tactics easier for the navigator. Several navigator's tasks require knowing compass heading and knotmeter speed such as solving true wind computations, figuring set and drift from GPS values of COG and SOG, and if you have speed and heading at hand you do not have to keep asking for it from the cockpit. The never ending question of the navigator "What is your course?" can then be answered without disturbing anyone.

Keeping the desired course in print in view of the helmsman is another sort-of nav station issue to be solved. The value of having this written down on deck for quick reference cannot be over stressed. When the course change, cross out the old and write in the new. This will help everyone stay on course and be a quick reference if forgotten in fatigue or tension of quick steering in waves. In the old days of sailing they had elaborate mechanical or manual devices for recording the course called a *course box*, always posted in direct view of the helmsman.

Unless it is intended for decoration, the barometer should be mounted in the nav station in clear view of someone standing next to the chart table—this is where most crew stand when filling in the logbook. To be of any value at all you must be able to look straight onto the barometer dial to minimize parallax, and most aneroid devices must be tapped gently to get an accurate reading—the exceptions being instruments like the Fischer Precision Aneroid Barometers that are essentially friction free. Generally one is looking for small changes in pressure and you simply can't gauge these from an angle, leaning over obstructions. It should also have a flashlight mounted next to it for nighttime reading. Again, if it is not convenient to get readings from it, logbook entries of pressure will be of little value. A well positioned barometer can be valuable even for inland day sailing or racing.

A rack for the sextant case is vital for offshore work and can be very valuable for inland and coastal sailing as well. Distance off and precision position fixing from vertical and horizontal sextant angles are important practical techniques in navigation that do not get used much, in part because most boats don't have a sextant handy. The techniques are easy to learn and apply. Even if a sextant is on board it is often buried. One solution is a convenient rack for the box, or better still some arrangement that mounts the box itself to the bulkhead. I have often found that the bulkhead between nav station and quarter berth is a good place to mount such a rack. The sextant is then inside the quarter berth, but high enough to not take up useful space, and easy to reach standing next to the nav station.

With the box mounted, after you take the sextant out, you do not have to worry about storing the box with only one hand free. A sextant sight to measure the angular height of a hill is then just as convenient as taking a bearing to it. A bearing and a sextant height gives you a fix. If this hill is the only thing in sight you have just done a nice piece of navigation.

For extended sailing, it pays to have headphone adaptors on all radios. This way the navigator can listen to weather reports without disturbing the off watch. It's also very helpful to have a built in tape recorder, or a rack for your personal tape recorder near the radios. You can then tape weather broadcasts. If reception is poor you need the tape to replay several times to get the message. Other times you may be busy or needed on deck. You can have the tape set up and the radio tuned, and then just turn things on when your wrist alarm goes off, and go back to whatever duty calls. Or you can ask someone to turn on the tape and radio at a particular time and let you sleep.

One thing I learned the hard way a long time ago was the value of a small, battery-operated nav station fan. Its purpose is simply to help cool off the navigator in hot weather. And before you start hollering wimp, wimp, wimp, let me give an ocean racing scenario from back in the days when we actually navigated by cel nav. It's 90° on deck in the Tropics with a nice breeze, but it is well over 100° below decks with no breeze. Eight sailors have been living in a 9 x 25 x 6-foot space for 12 days with no laundry service, a forgotten can of frozen orange juice somehow got misplaced in a locker and exploded one week ago, the boat is pitching and rolling in the Trades. The other seven crew are on deck having a great time in the fresh air, on their way to setting an elapsed-time record that will last 20 years—but the navigator is below decks with head spinning in the wooze, working out sun sights that must be done in an hour for the afternoon position report. Now wouldn't you grant this poor devil a small fan? §

Nav Station Supplies

- Penlight style flashlight (for the pencil holder)
- Pencils and sharpener (well tested ahead of time)
- Dividers (ultra light speed bow is top choice by far)
- Parallel Rules (15" clear plastic is popular)
- 360° square protractor (multiple uses and vector solutions)
- 18" ruler or P72 type (for extending lines and more)
- Weems rolling plotter (when it works, it works well)
- Erasers (pencil type and larger gum type)
- Large post-office rubber bands (for organizing things)
- Industrial Velcro (for improvised mounting of things)
- Highlight markers (several colors)
- Sharpie pens (fine point and bold, several colors)
- Post-its (for notes to yourself)
- Navigation notebook (for personal records)
- Some for of *course box*

OCEAN DEAD RECKONING

If we were guaranteed our GPS would always work, we would not have to do much more for ocean navigation. Unfortunately, we would never know if the GPS was right until the last day of the voyage—and we would be rightfully anxious about that throughout the voyage, because we know this cannot be guaranteed. On the other hand, we can guarantee that the sun will rise tomorrow and the stars will come out tonight, so if we learn celestial navigation we remove much of this anxiety, as well as learning other valuable skills such as how to check a compass offshore.

But there is always some luck involved in ocean voyaging, just as there is when going to the store to buy a loaf of bread. We cannot guarantee that our own atmosphere won't get in the way of our seeing the sun and stars when we need them most. We could wait out the overcast to find position and figure the next course, but that is not prudent policy. It could well be that this overcast is the forerunner of a storm we very much want to avoid, so we must keep moving. There are numerous reasons that days of delay could be detrimental.

The way we navigate between true position fixes (from cel nav, GPS, or any piloting fix) is called dead reckoning (DR). The name has likely evolved from the abbreviation ded for deduced reckoning, although there are those who grope around for an alternative origin. It means navigation by compass and log alone, aided by your knowledge of your boat and the waters you sail. Without actual position fixes, this is the way you carry on. In many senses, the highest goal of navigation training should be learning the skill of accurate DR.

The only way to learn how well you can do DR is to practice it. For this we need a log (odometer), a compass, and a logbook. In the learning process we can check our DR with the GPS on any waterway, since many of us do not get to sail in the ocean very often. But that is just to get started. The training must ultimately extend into the ocean because the crucial effect of big waves cannot be learned on inland waters. Also if your local waterway has much tidal current flow, it will have a notable effect on this exercise, but the practice remains invaluable.

The idea is simply whenever sailing, keep a careful logbook, and periodically compare your DR position to your GPS position, make a note of the differences (as explained below), then start over again. The more practice you get in various conditions, the more you learn.

Your compass should be checked and deviation removed. A typical binnacle mounted compass on a non-steel vessel should have no deviation if adjusted properly, but it has to be checked.

Sample Logbook				Computed values	
Time	Log	Course	Run	Total run	Total time
1120	606.8	045	0.0	0	0h 00m
1150	610.3	045	3.5	3.5	0h 30m
1259	618.4	310	8.0	11.6	1h 39m
1330	621.6	289	3.2	14.8	2h 10m
1535	638.4	022	16.9	31.6	4h 15m
				0.05 = 1.6	X0.5 =2.1
				1.5 x avg = 2.8	

Figure 1. *Sample logbook. This 4.25-hr run had an average speed of 31.6/4.25 = 7.4 kts, after which we found the DR wrong by 2.0 nmi. This is well within the suggested guidelines of 2.8 nmi in this example, where the time contribution and the distance contribution were comparable.*

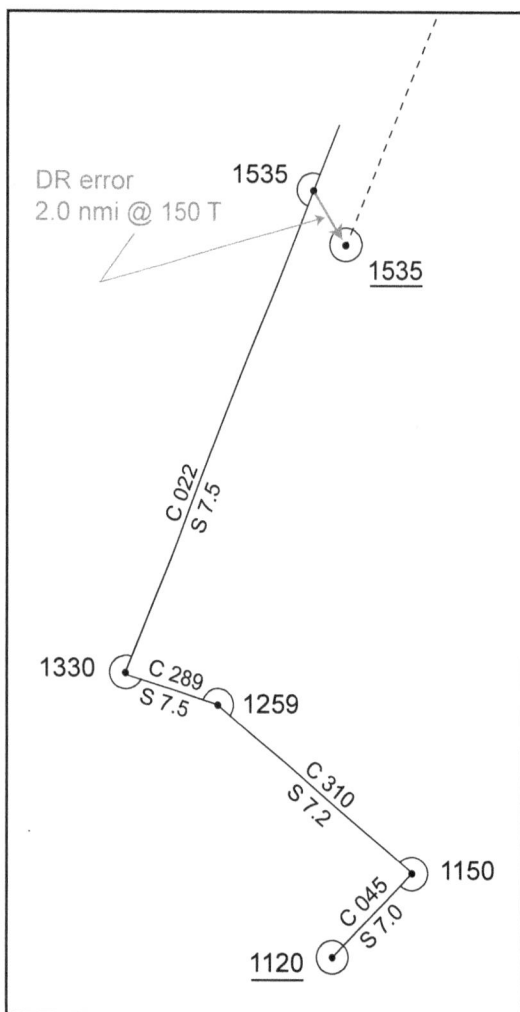

Figure 2. *Sample DR track plot. Based on the sample logbook, we start from a fix and 1120 and plot all course changes recorded in the logbook until the next fix at 1535. The difference between 1535 DR and fix (shown in red) is the DR error, 2.0 nmi in direction 150. By standard convention, fixes are plotted with full circles; DR positions with half circles. Each leg is labeled with course and speed. After 1535, the old DR track is abandoned and a new one started (dotted line).*

Your log and knotmeter should be calibrated (in calm air and still water) along a known distance run. The trip log is just another output from the knotmeter. Magnets in the impeller create a pulse each time it turns. The rate of the pulses is converted to speed in knots; the sum of the pulses is converted to distance run in nautical miles. Usually the software is such that the same calibration process corrects both.

Using a log for distance run is much more accurate than speed multiplied by time since our speed changes continually, especially in big waves. If you want to know your average speed, record the log every hour then subtract consecutive log readings.

The other key component to DR is the logbook. Make an entry (Time, Course, and Log) anytime something changes, and if nothing changes, make an entry every 4 hours—with an understood policy that no entry means nothing changed. The logbook will include much information, but the only data we need for DR are: the Time of course a change, the Course we changed to at that time, and the Distance Run on that course, which we get from subtracting successive Log entries.

As an example, let us assume we are headed off into the ocean and want to start this voyage with careful monitoring of our DR—the good policy we are recommending here. It is 1535 in the afternoon, and we have our GPS position for that time plotted on the chart. The last recorded position was at 1120 (4h 15m earlier). Then we update the DR track on the chart by plotting out all recorded course changes starting from the 1120 fix position, followed by the final run up to 1535 along the latest course line, and mark that DR position (usually a dot with a half circle). Now measure the range and bearing from the 1535 GPS position to the 1535 DR position. Let's say it was 2.0 nmi in direction 150 T. This is how much our DR was in error.

We now come to the main question at hand. Is this a big error or not? In other words, how well can we hope to do DR in the ocean? This is the key factor we need to know so we understand how our position uncertainty is increasing with time, which it inevitably will, when we are out of sight of land. The best next route to follow obviously depends on where we are now, but the best choice could also depend on how uncertain this starting point is. The more uncertain our present position, the more conservative our next route must be.

There are various ways to approach this. We studied this subject in depth when preparing the book *Emergency Navigation* (1980 to 1986). Details are in that text along with the analysis of several ocean passages, log entry by log entry. We are talking log and compass here, so nothing has really changed in the intervening 30 years, except we started out with nothing but cel nav for a reference, then we had Loran, then we had Transit Sat-Nav, and now we have GPS, but the key to good navigation and record keeping has not changed. In fact, the notable thing about Christopher Columbus—other than being a charlatan and one of the few nominally educated people of the time who did not know the radius of the earth—was his exceptional ability at DR. With nothing more than a chip log for speed, a sand glass for time, and a compass he did not understand at all, he still knew remarkably well where he was at all times (relative to his departure) based on his DR skills.

The rules of thumb we came up with are based on two things: how far you traveled and how long it took. Assuming your instruments are calibrated and you do everything right, you still have to assume that your DR position is growing uncertain in time by some 5% of the total distance run and the effect of an unknown error current of some 0.5 kts. We must consider both factors when estimating our DR uncertainty. Often one factor will dominate the other, and we can then focus on it. If they are about the same, then we might consider the total error as about 1.5 times their average.

This guideline says if you go out in the ocean, turn the engine off, and take all sails down, your position will become uncertain as if you were in a current of some 0.5 kts in a direction you do not know. After 24 hours you have to assume you could be anywhere within 12 nmi of where you think you are—maybe worse in some cases, maybe not so bad in others. This conclusion is based on wind drift studies, along with noting that the average ocean surface current flow around the world is some 0.5 kts as well.

Note that Pilot Chart current data should be interpreted as about ± 50%. A reported drift of 12 miles a day, could be anywhere between 6 and 18, with the higher estimate more likely if the wind has blown in the predicated current direction for several days, and the lower estimate if the wind has blown the opposite direction for several days.

Likewise if you zoom off at 30 kts, after you go 100 miles your DR position will be uncertain by some 5 miles or so—again maybe a bit more

or bit less depending on many factors. In this case the current drift of 1.7 nmi (0.5 x 3.3h) is small enough it could be neglected, because the errors add as the square root of the sum of the squares.

Though developed for ocean navigation, the limits given are a good guideline for all sailing, even across a large lake. Namely, without a real position fix, your DR position becomes uncertain by 5% of distance run within an error current of 0.5 kts.

In your practice underway, if you consistently do better than that, you are doing fine. If you cannot achieve that on average, then you are not optimized on your procedures or equipment.

To get a feeling for the magnitudes of these limits, note that a 6° right triangle has sides in the ratio of 1 to 10, and this proportion scales down forever and up to some 18°. That is, a 3° triangle has sides of about 1 to 20; a 12° triangle has sides of about 1 to 5, and so on. It is a powerful trick for navigators to know, with numerous applications.

Put into the context at hand, after you sail 100 nmi with a compass that is wrong by 6°, you will be off your intended track by 10 nmi. This is a 10% error; we are talking in our DR error estimates of 5%. So you can see that 5% DR is quite a good goal, namely it means you are steering what you record to within ±3°, with a log that is exactly right.

As for the log, when we strive for 5% we imply an indicated knotmeter speed of 7.0 is guaranteed to be right to within about 0.35 kts. This is a conservative goal, which is easy to achieve with calibration, so we see the main factor in DR accuracy is usually course made good.

The saving grace, meaning why this is not quite as difficult as it might appear, is we are assuming we have taken all systematic errors into account, i.e. we correct for compass error, current, leeway, and helm bias as best we can. In this case, the remaining errors are likely to be random, just as well to the left as to the right, so they tend to cancel.

Those errors that do not cancel, but in fact show up consistently, provide valuable information. If we find, for example, that regardless of tack or gibe, we find ourselves set to the south as if we were in a current of 0.3 kts, then we have learned that whatever estimates we have made for the current were off by that amount. Then we can add this to our subsequent corrections. Likewise, compass or log errors will show up as a consistent offset, which can likewise then be accounted for.

Sailing into the wind, you will find that your progress to weather will not be what you expect. The logged distance run will be about right, but your track will be offset downwind some 5° to 10° from what you expected, even with an esti-mated leeway correction—and it might not be the same on each tack, depending on the waves.

In any event, this type of analysis of compar-ing your fix positions with the corresponding DR positions and thinking in terms both percentage of distance run and an error current will help you unravel what is ailing your DR and prepare you for a time when you might not have the fixes to fall back on. An example is shown in Figure 2. §

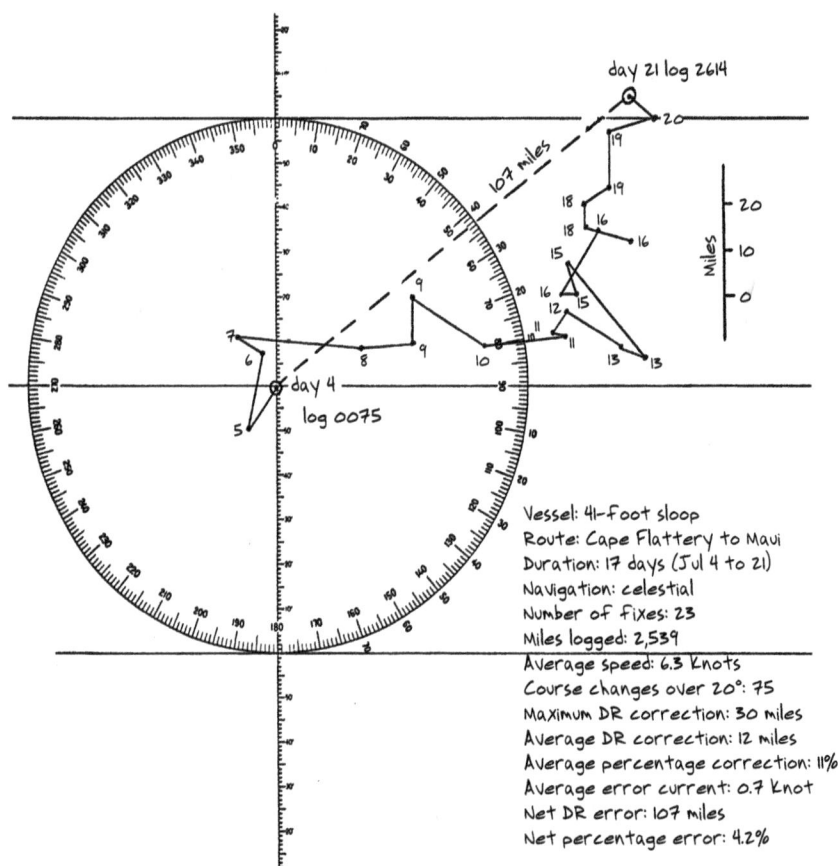

day 21 log 2614

107 miles

day 4
log 0075

Miles

Vessel: 41-foot sloop
Route: Cape Flattery to Maui
Duration: 17 days (Jul 4 to 21)
Navigation: celestial
Number of fixes: 23
Miles logged: 2,539
Average speed: 6.3 knots
Course changes over 20°: 75
Maximum DR correction: 30 miles
Average DR correction: 12 miles
Average percentage correction: 11%
Average error current: 0.7 knot
Net DR error: 107 miles
Net percentage error: 4.2%

Figure 2. *Vector plot of DR errors for an ocean passage made by cel nav alone in 1982. Individual DR errors are plotted sequentially to show how the vessel would progressively have gone off course if these correc-tions had not been made. Starting from day 4, the error on day 5 was 11 nmi in direction 215, then on day 6 it was 17 nmi in direction 012, and so on. If no fixes had been taken on this voyage, the boat would have been 107 miles off position at log reading 2614. Even though the individual errors averaged some 11% (taking into account distance covered on each leg), the net error was only 4%, which shows how random DR errors tend to cancel out over a long run—in part because these DR errors also reflect errors in the celestial fixes. The average DR error current was 0.7 knot (taking into account time spent on each leg), which is somewhat higher than is typical for a sailboat keeping a careful DR log—the winds were unusually erratic for this trip.*

This error log and another like it are analyzed and discussed in detail in Emergency Navigation, *and the actual celestial navigation of the whole voyage in presented as a training exercise in the forthcoming* Hawaii by Sex-tant *(Starpath Publications, 2013).*

KNOW YOUR LIMITS!

Mariners who sail both US inland and coastal waters are required to know one set of boundary limits—the ones that mark the jurisdiction of the US Inland Navigation Rules. These boundaries are called Demarcation Lines; they are specified at the back of the USCG printing of the Navigation Rules. On the inland side of these Lines, the US Inland Rules apply; seaward of these lines the COLREGs (International Rules) apply. Lights, sounds, and maneuvering rules are different in these two regions.

Sailing farther off shore, and in particular when approaching a foreign country, we are obligated to know about other limits, those generally referred to as marking the territorial sea of the country we approach. They are defined by the United Nations Convention on the Law of the Sea (www.un.org/Depts/los/index.htm) as a belt of coastal waters extending 12 nautical miles from the baseline of a coastal state, which separates the territorial sea from the nation's internal waters. The territorial sea is regarded as the sovereign territory of the state, although foreign ships (both military and civilian) are allowed innocent passage through it. When adjacent countries have overlapping territorial waters, the usual convention is to draw the boundary halfway between their baselines.

Innocent passage means—besides the obvious prohibitions on military or commercial activities of any kind—that you traverse the sea without entering the nation's internal waters, and that no cargo or personnel leaves or enters your vessel, and no fishing is allowed. The broad catch-all is Article 19, Part 2 (l): "…nor any other activity not having a direct bearing on passage."

The baselines used (by the US and other nations) are not defined the same way as the US Demarcation Lines, which are usually all coastal waters and point to point along the headlands marking entrances to what are called the Inland Waters. Baselines, in contrast, mark the boundary between the territorial sea and the internal waters of a country. Baselines are typically defined as the low-water line along the coast with extensions across headlands or sometimes following the tide lines into large bays, but there are variations. In fact, the US at one point used a fixed 3-nmi limit as marking its baseline, but technically this is no longer used, though some state and other legal jurisdictions still use that definition and consequently it is often referred to on nautical charts.

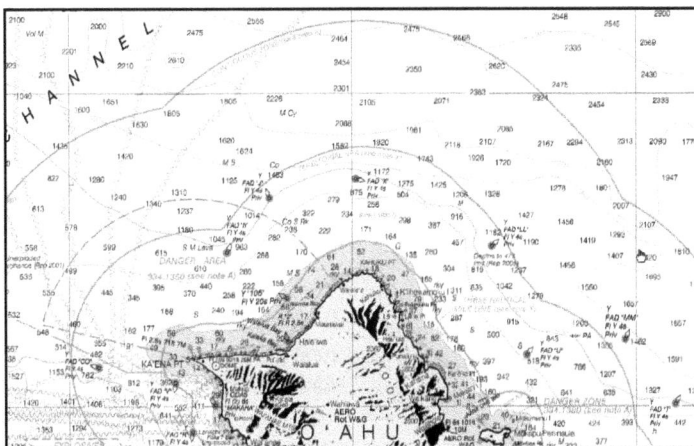

Figure 1. *Oahu*

The UN has on record a list of the waypoints that each country uses to establish its baseline.

There is also an important document at UN-LOS link called "Suspension of Innocent Passage," which states for each country the restrictions they have placed on the transit of foreign vessels into their territorial waters. These are typically temporary restrictions to account for military exercises, but they can also be notices of claims in disputed waterways. In any event, once across the baseline there is no innocent passage—you are in the country. According to the US Coast Pilot: "The United States has full sovereignty over its internal waters and ports as if they were part of its land territory," so other countries would likely have a similar interpretation.

Since we may not be able to check the primary UN sources, it is important for international sailing to check the International Notice to Mariners and other warnings at the NGA link at www. starpath.com/navpubs (the primary link changes often so we archive it here). These international notices are to be distinguished from the better known Local Notices to Mariners for US waters presented online at the USCG Nav Center (www. navcen.uscg.gov).

This fundamental 12-nmi limit for territorial seas is in the minds of many international sailors, but on closer look to the Law of the Sea that interpretation might not be conservative enough in some circumstances. According to the Law of the Sea, each country has the right to extend their 12-nmi territorial limit by another 12 miles with a contiguous zone. The special restrictions and rights a country can claim for their contiguous waters are specified in the Law, but we can use what the US claims as a guideline. The US contiguous zone was declared in a presidential proclamation in 1999, which in part stated:

"Within the extended contiguous zone, the Coast Guard may now board and search a foreign vessel suspected of smuggling drugs, carrying illegal immigrants, polluting the ocean, or tampering with sunken ships or other underwater artifacts, without first obtaining permission from the country where the vessel is registered. Previously, such action could be taken only within 12 miles of the coast."

Such a declaration in all effect extends the 12-nmi limit to 24-nmi, and since we can do it, there is no reason to think other coastal nations might not interpret their optional contiguous zone the same way. A check of the UN website for specific countries would answer that. Thus when planning routes past a foreign country you do not wish to enter, it could be prudent to keep this extended zone in mind with logged GPS positions. Some island nations use Archipelagic baselines, which effectively draws their baseline encircling their islands.

Other international limits exist such as the 200-nmi Exclusive Economic Zones, wherein a coastal nation has control of all economic resources, including fishing, mining, oil exploration, and any pollution of those resources, but these do not affect navigation. The claiming nation cannot prohibit passage or loitering above, on, or under the surface of the sea outside of its territorial waters. And there are special cases of these types of limits such as the US 9-nmi Natural Resource Boundary off the Gulf coast of Florida, Texas, and Puerto Rico, which involves laws just as complex as those referring to the US 3-nmi limit—both of more interest to oil companies, shoreline management, and conservation matters than to navigators. The 3-nmi limit pertains mostly to states' rights, which are defined in this document: http://coastalmanagement.noaa.gov/mystate/docs/StateCZBoundaries.pdf.

A related topic that does apply to navigation is a Restricted Zone marked on a nautical chart. These are often defined right on the chart, or there will be a number cited that directs you to the corresponding US Code. Their activation is usually noted in the Local Notice to Mariners. Territorial seas, contiguous zones, and baselines should also be marked on nautical charts, but they may not be updated on old charts. US charts do not show the baseline, but do show the 3-nmi limit, which can at least be used for a quick location reference line!

Looking ahead, one area of international boundaries that will come up in the news in the next year or so is the navigation rights to the Canadian Northwest Passage. Due to global warming, this will be adequately clear for shipping in the near future, though previously only routinely passable by icebreakers. Canada claims this route as their internal waters, whereas the US and all other maritime nations do not agree and claim rights of passage. Though as yet unresolved, I think we can be confident that it will be solved in a friendly manner, to the best interests of all involved.

At the time of writing, the Law of the Sea is also in the news as Iran threatens to close the Strait of Hormuz, in direct conflict with the Law. The territorial seas of Iran and Oman are divided by the mid point line through the Strait, with established Traffic Separation Lanes on the Oman side. Nevertheless, the entire Strait is legally (Article 38. Right of Transit Passage) open to navigation, and any attempt to block it is a violation of the Law. The Law is a treaty that Iran has not signed, but nevertheless, it would be an act that would gain immediate international response. One cannot be so confident that the outcome will be solved in a friendly manner—not to mention, that the bankers have already used this as an excuse to drive up the price of oil. §

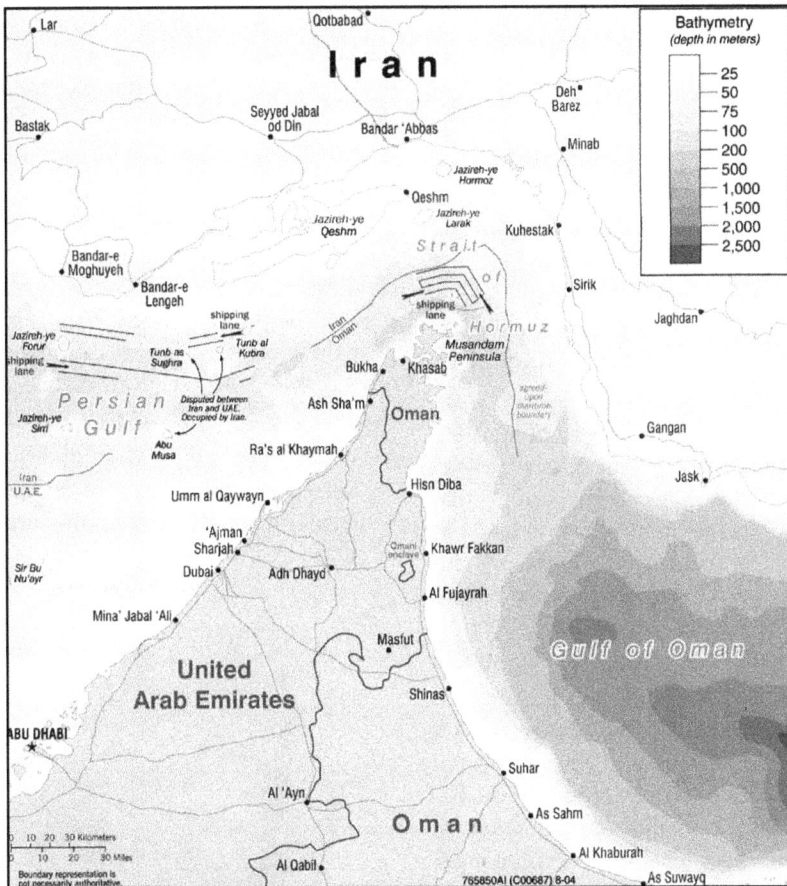

Figure 1. *Strait of Hormuz*

THE BOOKS OF CELESTIAL NAVIGATION

The practice of celestial navigation in the traditional manner, as opposed to using direct numerical solution by computer or programmed calculator, makes use of several printed publications, some periodical, some permanent. There are also options to each of these, so it is no surprise that an early question that comes up in the study of celestial navigation is what exactly are the publications I need to have on the boat as I pull away from the dock.

First a look at the basic answer, then a look at some options and additions.

(1) A *Nautical Almanac*. The almanac must be purchased once a year for about $30.

(2) A set of sight reduction tables. Of the several options, a popular one for sailors is Pub. 249, which comes in 3 volumes at $20 per volume. Volumes 2 and 3 are one time purchases; Vol 1 is published every 5 years, with each edition covering an 8-year period.

(3) Universal Plotting Sheets. Pad of 50 is $9. I would suggest two pads for an ocean crossing as they are also useful for weather routing—that is, if I am running in moderate NE wind and 300 miles ahead I expect the wind to go easterly and get stronger, I can use these sheets for a custom chart to layout the best way to approach the new wind considering my polar diagrams and known experience in the waves.

These are the basics that will do everything you need in any conditions, and thus the use of these is the focus of our cel nav course in the beginning. But there are significant options to be considered, especially as the basics become more familiar.

Almanac Options

The primary function of the *Nautical Almanac* is to tell us the latitude and longitude of the point on earth directly below all the celestial bodies, at each second of the day, throughout the year. This is called its "geographical position," the latitude of which is called "declination" and the longitude of which is called "Greenwich Hour Angle."

The data are computed and distributed by the US Naval Observatory (USNO) *Nautical Almanac* Office in collaboration with its British counterpart. Thus as far as options are concerned , there is an official government edition (orange cover, hardback) for $43 and a commercialized copy of the government edition (blue cover, paperback) that sells for $30. In principle, the latter is the same as the former with a few product advertisements added.

The math and science underlying these computations are not secret, so there are also other productions of the almanac data on line. Some are presented as free pdf files of the almanac data that can be printed. One source is www.navsoft.com; there are several. Any edition of the almanac other than the official government edition should be spot checked for accuracy with the original. The USNO link below is a good way to do this.

There are also publications called *Astronomical Almanac* and *Air Almanac*. Neither of these should be considered for marine use, although we do pe-

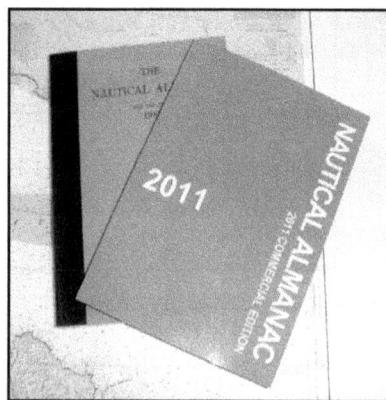

Figure 1. *The commercial edition of the* Nautical Almanac *(blue) is a copy of the government edition (orange), printed each year. These almanacs include a concise set of sight reduction tables.*

riodically still see misguided recommendations of the latter.

There are also PC programs that compute all the almanac data that will work long into the future, as well as (of course) mobile phone apps that do this. Again, all such products should be tested as noted. Some are free products others are sold.

There are also numerous online services that provide reliable almanac data. I mention just two: the US Naval Observatory: www.starpath.com/usno and the Frank Reed online almanac (among other resources he offers) at www.fer3.com.

There is also a printed *Long Term Almanac* that provides data for sun and selected stars out to 2050 by Geoffrey Kolbe. This small book does not include moon or planet data. Also it does not provide things like time of sunset, etc, but it does provide everything you do need for actual fixes from sun or star sights.

If cel nav is purely a back up system that you do not intend to use regularly, then this book would meet that need very nicely. It also includes a set of sight reduction tables, so it is a complete one-book long-term solution at a onetime cost of $20. If you do plan do to sights regularly then the traditional annual *Nautical Almanac* would be better for that, and this book should be considered as a back up for emergency use if you get stuck somewhere without access to a place to buy the new one or have one sent to you.

A reasonable solution is to take both the annual almanac and a copy of the *Long Term Almanac* that can be stowed with your back up gear.

Sight Reduction Options

There are many types of sight reduction tables, but they all serve the same function. Namely, you enter the tables with a Local Hour Angle (LHA), assumed Latitude (a-Lat), and declination (dec) and come out with the calculated altitude (Hc) and azimuth (Zn). In plainer words, if you know your latitude and the latitude over which a star circles the earth (its declination) and you know how far west of you it is at a specific time (its LHA), then sight reduction tables tell you how high it is in the sky (Hc) and the true direction to it (Zn) at that time. Mathematically speaking, they are tabulated solutions to triangles drawn

on the surface of the globe. You give them side-angle-side and they give you back the rest of the triangle's dimensions.

Besides Pub. 249 mentioned above there is also Pub. 229. The "Pub" in the title implies they are government publications of some agency. Originally it was the Navy, now some five agencies later it is NGA (National Geospatial Agency). They are a bit larger set of books that give the results with more precision (answers to 0.1′ compared to 1.0′ for Pub. 249). Use of Pub. 229 requires one volume for each 15° of latitude you plan to cover. Vol. 1 is 0° to 15°, Vol. 2 is 15° to 30°, Vol. 3 is 30° to 45°, and so on. These also sell for $20 each in paperback, again commercialized copies of government pubs. For most sailors, four volumes would cover all routes; for many others, just two or three volumes would do the job.

The use of Pub. 249 and Pub. 229 is about the same. There is one extra step required with Pub. 229 that is needed to get the extra precision, but all in all they are about the same to use, though laid out differently. Pub. 249 was originally developed for air navigation and that appears in its full title, but they remain in print because of their application by recreational mariners, not aviation.

Pub. 249 and Pub. 229 are called "inspection tables," because you enter them with a given LHA, Dec, and a-Lat and simply look up the corresponding Hc and Zn. There is just one correction for the arc minutes of the declination.

There is another type of sight reduction table called "concise tables," because they are very

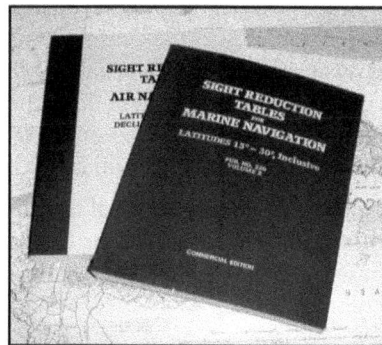

Figure 2. *The two popular inspection tables for sight reduction. Pub 229 is more precise than Pub 249 with just one extra correction to make.*

small—this is frankly not a good name for this type of table, but like other awkward terms in celestial navigation we are better off sticking to standard terms and not making up our own. A full set of the inspection tables is about 1,000 large pages of numbers (weighing about 8 lbs), whereas concise tables (there are several editions) are all about 30 small pages of numbers, about half the size of this magazine.

But if we are to get the same data from such concise (condensed) tables we have to pay a price, and that price is a bit more number crunching. Instead of a one step process with inspection tables, we have four entries into concise tables with some arithmetic in between. We end up with precision the same as Pub. 249, but it takes a bit longer to get it.

One set of concise tables stands out from the others because it is included in every official *Nautical Almanac*. Thus in principle we only need to buy an almanac to have everything we need, provided we do our sight reduction with its set of concise tables. These are called the NAO Sight Reduction Tables, with the letters from Nautical Almanac Office. Using the Starpath custom work form for these tables, the sight reduction goes very smoothly and does not take much longer than using Pub. 249.

As for recommendations for a printed set of inspection tables, the Pub. 229 is likely the best choice. It stands out because the alternative Pub. 249 requires that you do star sight reductions in a different manner from the other bodies, whereas with 229 everything is the same. Also the 229 results are more precise, which could matter if you want to do your very best and all other factors have been optimized. These other factors such as right choice of bodies, good sextant practice, correction for boat motion, etc are usually each one more important than the precision difference between 229 and 249, so unless you do everything else exactly right, this difference will not matter.

The best way to make a personal decision on this is try them all out, which can be done without purchase since they are all online. See www.starpath.com/navpubs.

I must mention the fact that we start our Starpath cel nav course using Pub. 249 (not 229) primarily because of the way the tables are laid out. The Pub. 249 page layout makes it easier to explain the sight reduction process and to offer more examples with fewer sample table pages. However, once anyone learns the sight reduction process, it is a simple matter to switch to any one of the sight reduction tables.

Alternatively, a paperless approach is to do all sight reduction with a calculator that is programmed for the task or a PC app of which there are many, including numerous free ones (see NIMA calculators at www.starpath.com/navpubs). Then practice once or twice with the NAO tables included in the almanac and consider that your back-up to the computer solution. Computed solutions contribute to better navigation because they are less prone to error and because they are so fast we tend to take many more sights. Cel nav programs can include both almanac and sight reduction functions as well as many other related features.

Extra Books for the Black Belts of Celestial Navigation

I mentioned the *Long Term Almanac* which is a back-up for no other source of almanac, but this book like the other almanacs assumes you have an accurate source of Universal Time (UTC). Without time you can get your latitude but not your longitude. To prepare for the loss of UTC would add another book to your list, namely The *Stark Tables for Clearing the Lunar Distance and Finding UTC from Sextant Observations*. This book was the subject of the August 2010 issue. This book tells how to measure and analyze the diagonal sextant distance between the moon and another celestial body along its path to obtain the correct UTC, and from this you can find your longitude. This adds a high level of independence to your boat as you no longer have to worry about losing accurate time.

If you want even more independence, there is one more small book to consider, which we call the *Lunar Almanac* in public and the "Doomsday Almanac" in private. With the *Stark Tables* you can find the correct time, but these tables assume you have an almanac with the required moon data. But moon data are typically published only once a year for the current year. The *Lunar Almanac* (Starpath Publications, 2013) expands this coverage to provide the required tabulated lunar distances long into the future. Thus with the package of the *Long Term Almanac*, *Stark Tables*, and *Lunar Almanac* you could find your way to any port in the world for the next 20 years, completely independent of all civilization, all computers, and all batteries.

(It would, of course, be better to have a sail boat than a power boat if this need should arise, and one would likely be headed toward the equator, away from the typical flow of the winds aloft, which could be transporting contaminants you would want to avoid.)

Again, these last three books are not required for routine celestial navigation. They are an ultimate backup package and a way to hone your skills as a celestial navigator by demonstrating your complete and enduring independence of all the aids we typically consider crucial to ocean navigation. §

Figure 3. *Kolbe's* Long Term Almanac *provides one-book ocean navigation till 2050, assuming you have correct time, otherwise use the* Stark Tables *and* Lunar Almanac *for longitude without time. The ultimate back-up collection.*

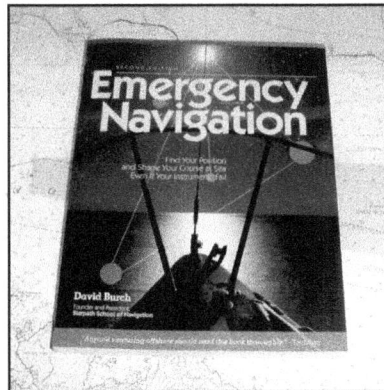

Figure 4. *Test your celestial skills underway or in the backyard by doing it all without instruments, as guided by this book, now celebrating its 25th birthday.*

"K" IS FOR COMMUNICATE

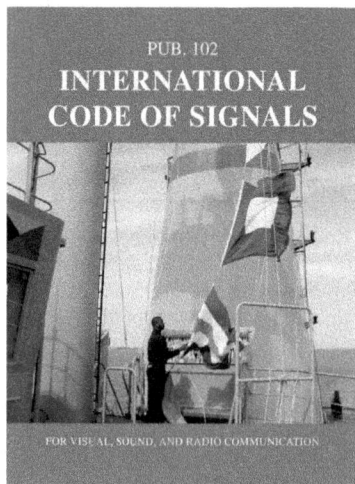

PUB. 102

INTERNATIONAL CODE OF SIGNALS

FOR VISUAL, SOUND, AND RADIO COMMUNICATION

K(dah dit dah) is a one letter code used in maritime communications to mean "I want to communicate." You can send this with Morse code by keying the mic or by sounding your air horn—or by flashing lights, or with signal flags, or just hoist the single code flag K (rectangle with left side yellow, right side blue). Or you could tap it out on the wall of your jail cell, or on your girlfriend's desk at work.

But how are you going to know that? And how are you going to reply? The answers are in a definitive little book called the *International Code of Signals — NIMA Publication 102*. These 157 pages tell you all you could ever want to know about communication by signals. A "K" followed by a "9," for example, means I want to communicate by VHF on channel 16. "K' followed by "4" means I want to use Morse code with flashing lights.

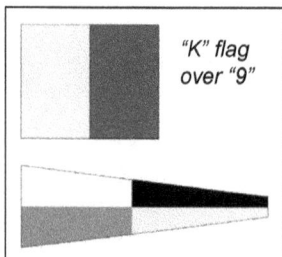

"K" flag over "9"

When you might be improvising your signals by tapping or blowing a horn, we learn from *Pub 102* that the noise you choose for the "dot" is the basic unit. A dash is then 3 units long, and the space between letters is one unit long.

Pub 102 is no longer printed by the U.S. government, but several commercial reproductions are available from $15 to $30. The International Maritime Organization (IMO) still offers their version in print at $129 for essentially the same book. In place of print distribution, NIMA (National Imaging and Mapping Agency, formerly the Defense Mapping Agency) offers the U.S. version online as a free pdf. See www.starpath.com/navpubs for a link to the NIMA source, which is somewhat of a moving target. There are other valuable resources at this link as well.

This book is an official statement of everything from the Morse code and phonetic alphabet on up to the less familiar double letter codes used in special circumstances. Rules and procedures for sending these letters by sound signals, waving your arms or flags, or by using flashing lights are all explained.

It includes an extensive list of one letter codes such as "K" mentioned above. Some of these we are already familiar with, but may not know it. "E" (dit) means "I am altering course to starboard" and "I" (dit dit) means "I am altering my course to port." Remember, these are *international* signals, so this signal would not mean "I intend to leave you on my starboard side" as it would on US Inland waters. The letter "S" (dit dit dit), however, means "I am operating astern propulsion" no matter where you are. We might like to think it means "I am backing up," but it does not. It means what it says: the engine is running and in reverse. It does not require you to be moving backwards.

Leaving aside the details of the Rules, (no matter how interesting!) we should return to the topic at hand, the code. You could sound that code on your horn, or by flashing lights at the vessel you are communicating with. It is valuable to

Alfa · —	Kilo — · —	Uniform · · —	1 · — — — —
Bravo — · · ·	Lima · — · ·	Victor · · · —	2 · · — — —
Charlie — · — ·	Mike — —	Whiskey · — —	3 · · · — —
Delta — · ·	November — ·	Xray — · · —	4 · · · · —
Echo ·	Oscar — — —	Yankee — · — —	5 · · · · ·
Foxtrot · · — ·	Papa · — — ·	Zulu — — · ·	6 — · · · ·
Golf — — ·	Quebec — — · —	SUBSTITUTES 1st Substitute	7 — — · · ·
Hotel · · · ·	Romeo · — ·	2nd Substitute	8 — — — · ·
India · ·	Sierra · · ·	3rd Substitute	9 — — — — ·
Juliett · — — —	Tango —	CODE	0 — — — — —

remember that you can supplement what we tend to think of as "sound signals" with flashing lights. Strong winds and big seas can be very noisy, but you can always see the lights. This is, of course, stated in the *Navigation Rules* themselves, not just in the code book.

We obviously don't know when we are going to need to use some form of code. It seems some ocean racing committees think it is less likely these days than it used to be. We used to have to carry the code book on every ocean race as part of the rules, as well as a full set of signal flags. Now I see at least one set of ocean racing rules that requires a satellite phone, but no mention at all of *Pub 102*.

This is a mistake. It is like requiring extra GPS batteries, but no sextant—a believe-it-or-not actual rule in one race. This is frankly poor seamanship. Granted, we are all slowly becoming more dependent on electronics and the electronics are becoming slowly more dependable, but once you push off from the dock and head across the ocean in a small boat, you raise the bar on self reliance and dependability.

The hallmark of good seamanship is good preparation. If we lose conventional communication we need a backup. It is a long shot that you

end up on a beach signaling an approaching aircraft to a safe place to land, or warning that this is not safe to land. Vertical versus horizontal waving of the arms is the difference between these totally opposite signals, which would be nice to see in print and not just in memory. Again, that is an extremely unlikely situation. But signaling a helicopter overhead in a bad storm that you need medical help when you do not have a radio working is, at least conceptually, less remote. The code flag "W" would convey that without other specifications. *Pub 102*, however, contains extensive medical code signals to be more specific.

Annex IV, Section 1 (f), of the *Navigation Rules* reminds us that "N" and "C" flown together means "I am in distress and need assistance," implying this should be recognized by all mariners as a distress call. It also states this is found in the *International Signal Code*.

But there are mundane code applications as well. I recall an ocean race where a yacht's radio was not functioning properly, but when it keyed its mike it made a distinct noise, though no words could be discerned. In this race, like most, you must report your position every day at a fixed time for all of the fleet to hear. If you fail to do so, you get penalized in time for each day missed.

You can now guess the answer! They keyed in their position in Morse code every day. It was painful to hear and record, but they met their obligation. The radio control vessel did the translation and relayed it, much to the relief of many navigators, though some, as I recall, took it on as a personal challenge to decipher the messages.

Which is of course reminiscent of Amelia Earhart. It is often reported that she and her navigator Fred Noonan did not know (or were not proficient at) Morse code. And on top of that, they had left the required radio equipment off the plane to save weight. This would have made sending and receiving easier, but reports are that she could indeed key her mic and that much be heard. So if she had some equivalent of *Pub 102* on board, she might have been able to send her location, and may have been saved.

These days life is rather simpler. Now you can get an app for your iPhone—and almost certainly multiple other phones as well in the near future—that does all the Morse translation for

—INTERNATIONAL—
Sound and Light Signals

RULE 37
Distress Signals
When a vessel is in distress and requires assistance she shall use or exhibit the signals described in Annex IV to these Regulations.

DISTRESS SIGNALS
72 COLREGS

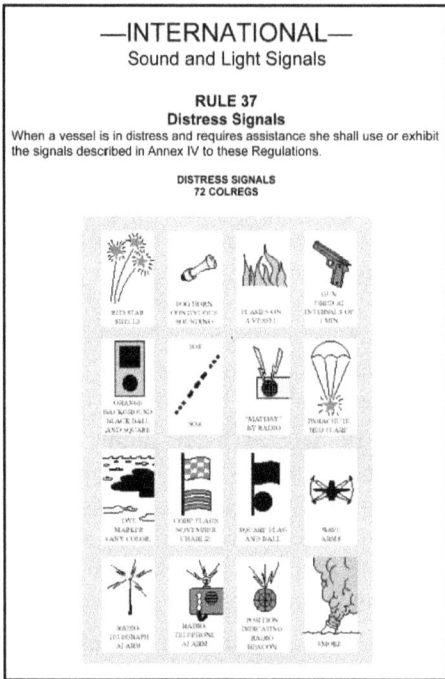

you. Just type in what you want to say, and the code comes out—in characters, or audio, or flashing lights. For the PC there are even apps that go the other way, and decode what you receive. (In passing, I cannot mention *iPhone* apps without a plug for Philippe Kahn's super program called MotionX GPS. It is a look at the future.)

Pub 102 is only 2 megabytes, so the entire text can fit in your phone. Idle reading when waiting in line could prove useful... and if that gets boring, you can switch over and read the *Navigation Rules*; they are only 1.3 Mb. This is the most important book in navigation. If you know and obey the Rules, it is statistically near impossible to be involved in a collision—in that, essentially every collision involves the violation of at least one Rule by *both* vessels.

Whenever I have the opportunity to talk about communications at sea there are another couple items that also always come to mine, beyond the main topics covered elsewhere in this issue. I will mention two.

If you are the captain or navigator, teach other crew members to use the radios. If you are a crew member, ask to learn to use the radios. I know of ocean passages where only the navigator and captain knew how to use the SSB radio and sat

phone. This should be part of your routine station bill training.

In any ocean passage there will end up being a sequence of crucial communications to make during the day. Often you can make a written schedule of these before your departure, which could be of great benefit. If you do not start off with one, you will end up with one in a few days, so it is best to make up as much of it as you can before leaving.

The things that go into this schedule are the times of weather broadcasts, fax and voice, as well as time to check in or report your position, or to make some other planned communication, such as listening in on a cruising network. You also need reminders to record your weather observations (at least wind and pressure) at the synoptic times of 00z, 06z, 12z, and 18z (z=GMT). These data are needed to evaluate the weather maps.

This communications schedule is not so easy to make as it might seem because some of event times will be in different time zones from your vessel's time.

Also you have to interpret what you have on the list. If your vessel is keeping zone 7 time, then the weather map valid at 12z will be valid at 5am on your watch time, and this map might be broadcast at 1530z, which means you would record it at 0830 ship time. And so on. The cruiser's net you want to listen to might be broadcast every day at 1500 on zone 5, so you have to tune in every day at 1300.

Then you better put on the schedule when to charge the batteries, so the radio will work when you need it. Again, it seems a simple thing to make this communications schedule, but it is not so simple. And it does not seem that crucial to have such a written schedule at first, but you soon learn it is very crucial to your navigation.

But even with all this organization and all the state of the art communications, we must still do some basic navigation study if we are to travel around the world by boat.

In the recent news we learn of a high tech racing yacht with all the state of the art navigation and communication equipment in place and working as it headed toward the start of the Dubai to Muscat Yacht Race from its home port in Bahrain.

TABLE OF MORSE SIGNALING BY HAND FLAGS OR ARMS

Note: The space of time between dots and dashes and between letters, groups or words should be as such to facilitate correct reception

The Iranian island of Sirri is 32 miles off the rhumb line course to the yacht club, which put the territorial waters of Iran just 20 miles to port as they pass. We can only guess that this must have been very well known, because even the Notice to Race issued 6 months earlier warned all participants to avoid the territorial waters of Iran. The race's Sailing Instructions even stated yachts would be disqualified if they entered Iranian waters. A route well south of the rhumb line would have seemed more prudent in light of all these warnings. Not to mention the value of paying attention to where you are.

It is rather like sailing down past Cuba, and not knowing if you are within 12 miles of Cuba, but just a lot more serious. They entered Iranian waters and were arrested. Thankfully, they were released within a week, but one fears to think of what could have happened as a result of this navigational error. At the least it cost them the race, and as self-described "full-time professional racing sailors" this is not good advertising.

Which brings us back to *Publication 102*, whose preface emphasizes "The Code is intended to cater primarily for situations related to safety of navigation and persons, especially when lan-guage difficulties arise." Their situation is just what the book is made for!

If it had turned out (which it did not) that none of their radios were working, they might have been frantically flipping through the pages trying to figure out why the Iranian gunboat changed a signal code flag from just "L" to "S" over "L."

The CFRs tell us several places that we are obligated to know that code flag "L" means you "You should stop immediately." Fisheries enforcement vessels dealing with foreign vessels often have occasion for this signal. Adding the flag "S" ratchets things up a level. S over L means "Do not scuttle. Do not lower boats. Do not use wireless. If you disobey I shall open fire on you."

Then when you are being towed into jail you will have some time to practice tapping your cup on the deck. §

ICOS Plus
By Mintaka Research, LLC

An iOS app of an interactive Pub 102 along with all weather and sailboat racing signals is described at www.starpath.com/icosplus

---

46 CFR 108.713
Each vessel on an international voyage which is required to carry a radiotelegraph or radiotelephone installation in accordance with Chapter IV of the Safety of Life at Sea Convention, 1960, must carry the *International Code of Signals.*

SOLAS, Chapter 5, Reg 21

Adds to the above that "The Code shall also be carried by any other ship which, in the opinion of the Administration, has a need to use it"

LUNARS!

For the celestial navigator who has everything, they are a challenge, when met, that will put you into the company of Bowditch, Cook, Vancouver, and the like.

Some long while ago when I had more money and time than I do now, I took up the sport of flying. In the process, an instructor convinced me that to be a really good pilot, safe and versatile, I should take training in aerobatics. This led to some exciting hours behind "the stick" of a Champion Citabria, strapped into a parachute, with a cable at hand that would release the entire side of the plane with a single pull. It was for sure a different kind of flying than I was used to, and it for sure made me a better pilot—even though in the end I did not pursue either type of flying.

The aerobatics of celestial navigation is called "the lunar distance method for finding longitude without time," or *lunars* for short. And now the instructor is saying, if you learn lunars you will become a far better celestial navigator in your routine work, and on top of that you will be prepared for any of the various doomsday scenarios such as no more GPS, no more radio time signals, no more computers, no more iPhones. In fact, with a few special tables printed out and stowed, you could navigate with your sextant alone to any point on earth for the next 20 years, even if there were no more civilization left at all.

Granted, that is rather overdoing it in the back-up department, even for a prudent mariner, but there is no doubt that your routine cel nav will shine in the light of your new skills as a *lunarian*, which can be mastered, sitting in a chair in your backyard, without a view of the sea horizon. Lunar skills are universally considered the hallmark of the best celestial navigators.

The opportunity to carry out this technique in the traditional manner without computers has recently become very convenient with a new publication of the *Stark Tables for Clearing the Lunar Distance and Finding Universal Time by Sextant Ob-*servations — *Including a Convenient Way to Sharpen Celestial Navigation Skills while on Land*. This book has rejuvenated this procedure worldwide and with it celestial navigation in general.

Celestial navigation is a way to find your latitude and longitude using a sextant to measure

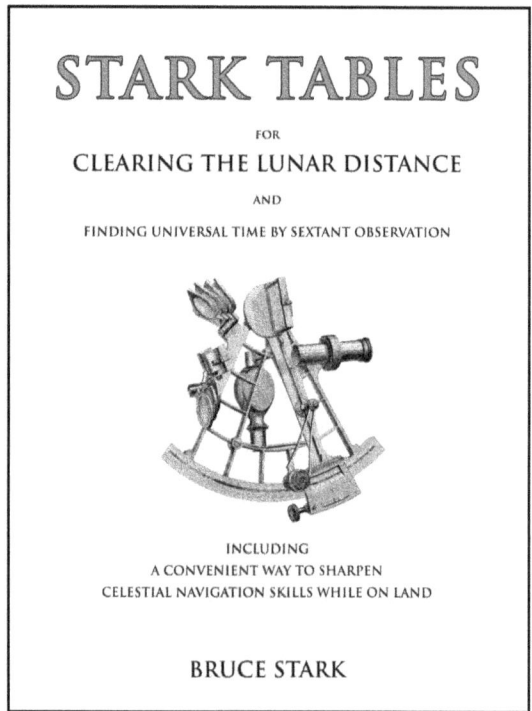

Figure 1. *The new, revised edition from Starpath Publications (June, 2010), available online or in nautical book stores.*

the angular heights of celestial bodies above the horizon. It has been used by mariners at sea and explorers on land for three hundred years, and it is still used today as a dependable backup to modern electronic navigation. You cannot get an Unlimited Ocean Masters license from the USCG without knowing routine celestial navigation.

Routine celestial navigation relies upon accurate time (Universal Time) to find the longitude of a position (latitude does not require time).

Advanced celestial navigators, however, can find longitude without knowing the time using the technique of Lunar Distance. In this technique, the sextant is used to measure the angular distance between the moon and another celestial body along its path. Since this distance slowly changes as the moon moves eastward though the Zodiac constellations, it can be used to find the time of day that is needed to complete the longitude determination.

Cook did some of this) and most crucially, it had to be proven that someone other than the inventor (John Harrison) could manufacture them.

The production and dependability of the instruments was getting sorted out by the early 1800s, but they were still very expensive, especially since one was not enough to guarantee the right time. If it is wrong, you don't know it. Likewise, two are not enough. To know the time accurate to the second, over a long voyage away from

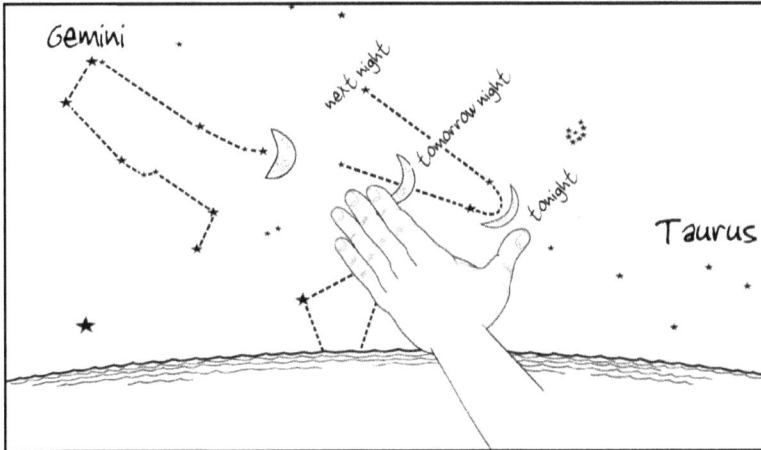

Figure 2. *The moon circles the earth (360°) in about 30 days, so viewed at the same time each night, the moon moves eastward through the stars at a rate of about 12°/day. The moon's path is through the stars of the Zodiac.*

There are several reasons this valuable technique has not been part of routine celestial navigation for over a hundred years. First and foremost, it is not needed, so long as the navigator has accurate time, which is readily at hand these days. The history of lunars is inseparable from the history of timekeeping at sea, because the achievements in astronomy needed to predict the location of the moon accurate enough to do lunars came about at almost the same time as the invention of accurate sea going watches, which would ultimately cause the demise of the lunar method of finding longitude.

Dependable seagoing watches were invented in the mid 1700's. It is a famous story, made popular in Dava Sobel's book called *Longitude*—a boon to the public knowledge of navigation history, despite some poetic license and struggle with details. But the invention alone did not make it a practical solution. It needed testing (Captain

civilization, you need at least three watches. That is still true today if you want to be independent of radios and GPS.

I say "watch," meaning a portable clock, but should say "chronometer." A chronometer is just a watch that gains or loses time at a constant rate. The actual magnitude of the rate (say it gains 0.3 seconds per day) does not matter, so long as it is constant. With a known constant rate and date set, you can always figure the correct time. By the mid to late 1800s chronometers, though still expensive, were in reach of most ship's captains. Chronometers remained relatively expensive all the way up to the days of the Bulova Accutron in the early 1960's. Then the prices started down. Now essentially any quartz watch is a chronometer, and three topnotch, waterproof models is less than $100. But they still have to be tested, preferably over the full temperature range expected. Put them inside an electric blanket and then inside the fridge for a couple months each, as you monitor their rates.

With good timekeeping practice, we really should not lose accurate time in normal conditions, especially since we have accurate time from every GPS satellite, and there are numerous radio broadcasts of GMT, now called Universal Time (UT). But it is not unheard of, nor unimaginable. And prudent good seamanship means considering things beyond normal conditions.

All electronics are vulnerable at sea. Watchbands are more vulnerable than the watches in many cases, which can lead to the lost of a watch. Plus they take batteries. Do you know how long your watch battery will last? Do you take spare watch batteries when you go offshore? If your watch stops with a dead battery and you replace it offshore, what time do you set it back to? Does that turn your 3 chronometers into two?

And, there is always Doomsday. Those of us who thought Doomsday was somehow more remote after the fall of the Soviet Union, are day by day, waking up to smell the coffee. The world has not evolved as we might have guessed it would. Two days ago, one nuclear power literally threatened a neighbor with total destruction, after torpedoing one of its ships killing 48 sailors. The concept of nuclear proliferation and its dire consequences are more and more a part of the daily news, not less. It is way too early to write off Doom.

Nevertheless, the main reason most navigators do not do lunars is they have accurate time and do not need to—that is, if we rule out the even bigger reason, namely, most navigators do not know the technique exists. It was not covered in any books they used.

Navigators who are aware of lunars and would like to learn them, have had other challenges. First, the special diagonal sextant sights are more difficult than normal cel nav sights, which are always measured straight up from the horizon, and the results must be more accurate. This requires learning to use the sextant to its very limits. But this challenge is part of the reward. The practical limit to sextant accuracy is about ±0.1' of arc. Without much practice or good instruction, navigators might average some 3 or 4 times that limit, or even a bit worse. To be successful with

lunars, however, you must practice until you can approach the instrument limit routinely, even using the sextant in the awkward diagonal manner. Higher-powered monocular telescopes help with this. Precomputing the lunar distance ahead of time is also helpful.

There are navigators who do lunars with plastic sextants, but this takes even more special care, and average results are not as good as with metal sextants. Put another way, it would make you even better if you could do them with plastic sextants, and in any event it is way to see how the whole process works without the investment of a metal sextant. The author's booklet How to Use Plastic Sextants (starpath.com) is required reading for this endeavor, besides raising the general quality of all sextant sights, metal and plastic.

As an aside to celestial navigators, another great benefit is you will learn a new technique for finding the sextant's index correction (what we call at Starpath the solar method). This is much more accurate than the conventional procedure using the horizon, plus it contains a self-consistency check because it measures the sun's semi-diameter, which can be looked up in the almanac. This correction measurement is not taught in modern textbooks that do not include lunars.

The other issue has been the challenge of analyzing the lunar distance to get longitude once it has been measured accurately. The government tables that used to do this went out of print in the early 1900s and it is essentially impossible to use old ones for modern sights. There are computer programs and Internet sites that have computed the solutions for many years, but reliance on a computer or an Internet service for a back up procedure is completely incongruous. Thus there has not been a logical role for lunars outside of academic and historic study beyond a select group of sextant experts who use it to maintain their prowess. That is, until now.

The *Stark Tables* are a modern take on this venerable problem, but as lunar expert George Huxtable, FRIN, put it, "Captain Cook would have relished using the *Stark Tables*, had they been available to him then." They are an ingenious application of the same basic methods of the 1700s, but they are easier to use. Doing all the paperwork by hand, filling out custom forms, you can go from a measured lunar distance to the correct time and your longitude in about 15 minutes, without even needing a calculator. You can measure the lunar distance any time of night that is convenient, since you do not need to see the horizon. The altitudes of the bodies above the horizon (which cannot be seen in the middle of the night) are needed in the process, but they can be computed from tables to sufficient accuracy from a DR position. Likewise, the sun and moon are frequently in good view for the sights throughout the day.

Robert Eno in a Navigator's Newsletter review said "It is remarkable in this day when the very survival of celestial navigation seems in question, that an individual should suddenly appear on the scene and present to the world such a brilliant piece of work. Stark has rendered a great service to the celestial navigation community."

The accuracy achievable depends on the quality of the sights and the choice of bodies. The *Stark Tables* explain how to choose the best companion. You want one in line with the motion of the moon, so the change in lunar distance with time is the greatest. The sun is good just about any time it is in view with the moon and within reach of the sextant. At night you want bodies (star or planet) perpendicular to a line drawn across the horns of the moon. It can be on either side. The *Stark Tables* include a way to evaluate the quality of your choice in this regard, and they also provide detailed instructions on taking the sights.

You can't expect to get lunar longitudes as precise as you can with accurate time, but they will be quite serviceable. A 1 arc minute sextant error (1.0') in the distance measurement will cause about a 2 minute error in the time when using the best companion bodies. If you can achieve 0.5' accuracy, you improve to 1 minute error in time, which corresponds to a 15' error in longitude. This in turn corresponds to about 15 nmi in the Tropics or about 10 nmi at the latitude of Seattle. Navigators skilled in this method can generally get down to averaging closer to 30 seconds error in time.

If you surf around the web looking into the topic online, you will find far more discussion of the details and complexities of the process than you will find discussion of its practical use today.

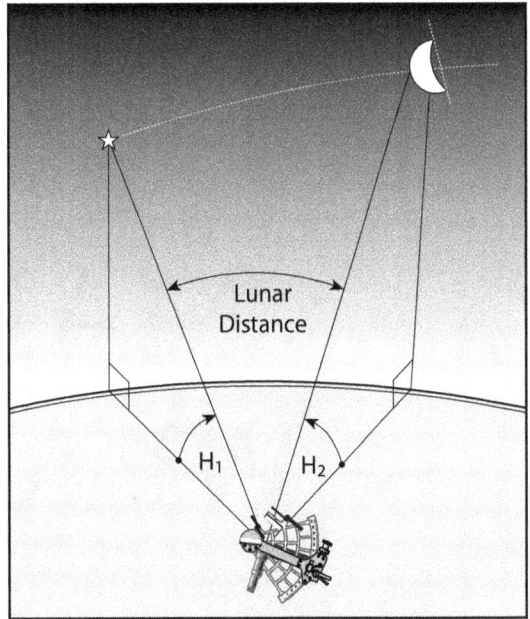

Figure 3. *Lunar distance is the angle between the edge of the moon and another celestial body along the Zodiac. The sextant can reach out to about 120°, though sights half this range or less are easier to do. The angular heights of the bodies perpendicular to the horizon are used in the analysis, but these values can be computed if an almanac is available.*

And sure enough, there are many nuances to the process. These details, however, are all accounted for in the *Stark Tables*, so they can be treated as we do so many other navigation tables. Just use them for their practical value without worrying about the rigors of their physical and mathematical foundations. In the end the test is very simple. You stand at a known place with a watch set to some unknown error, and see if you can find out where you are. If it works for you there, it will work for you at sea. It is one of the most rewarding navigation exercises you can do.

With the *Stark Tables* in your nav station, you no longer have to fear losing power to your electronic navigation aids, nor are you dependent on accurate time from any official broadcast. It is a small investment in time and energy that greatly expands your skills and preparation for the unexpected. For all we know, a volcano in Iceland might suddenly erupt and wipe out all of the air travel in Europe in a matter of days.

MARINE
WEATHER

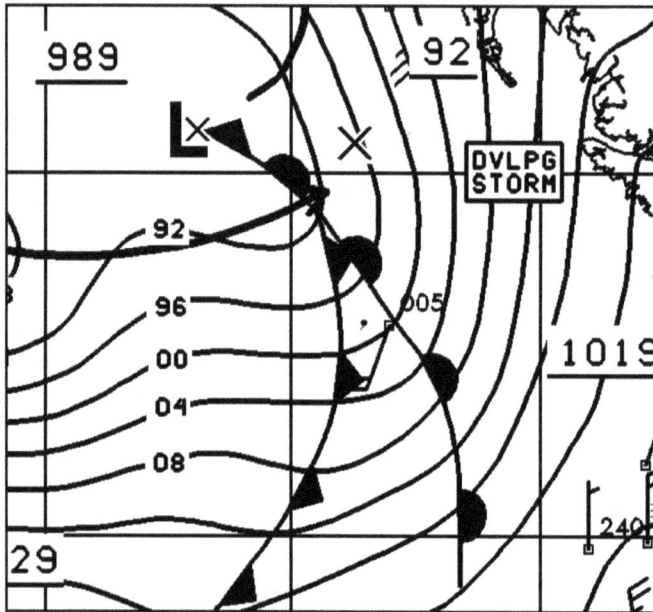

BAROMETER TACTICS

Even in these modern times of satellites and Internet weather data, the atmospheric pressure measured with the ship's barometer remains the most important predictor of weather changes at your location. To evaluate present weather or to forecast coming weather, we need accurate barometric pressure. Wind speed and direction changes are also important to know for the best forecast, but pressure remains the most crucial, in the most circumstances.

It may seem a surprise, but in modern times the use of accurate pressure is a new concept. We have been taught that the only thing that matters is the pressure trend: is it going up or going down; is the change fast or slow.

But this was not at all the case in the golden age of sailing of the 19th century, and even before then during the great age of discovery. In those days mariners routinely measured accurate pressure using mercury barometers, as extremely difficult as it was. Every ocean voyage in those days was a gold mine of pressure data that led very early on to a remarkably good picture of the average worldwide atmospheric pressure patterns. This allowed scientists like William Ferrel (1817-1891) to explain the global wind patterns: dol-

drums, trade winds, subtropic Highs, and prevailing westerlies, which in turn was a key stepping stone in the evolution of meteorology. Ferrel, by the way, was also the first person to apply what we call the Coriolis Force to the flow of wind, and he was also the first to present what we now call the Buys Ballot Law for locating the direction to low pressure, among several other remarkable achievements.

Sea captains in those days had broad knowledge of atmospheric pressure. If they were sailing in the Tropics and the pressure dropped from 1013 to 1010 mb, they knew a storm was on the way, even if they did not see it in the clouds or detect it in the wind. Even more important, they also knew that this same observation in Boston Harbor would not signify anything at all.

Nineteenth century captains were always aware of the pressure pattern they were sailing in. North of the Equator, they called a pressure drop on a starboard tack a "red-ink warning" because they knew that on a starboard tack they should be sailing into higher pressure. See Figure 1.

A rising barometer on a port tack, on the other hand, was a particularly good sign of improving weather, because the barometer should be dropping on a part tack unless the pressure pattern itself is rising. It is not the gospel, but generally fair weather comes with higher pressure, whereas strong winds, clouds and rain come with lower pressure.

Rules on pressure trends and wind shifts persisted into modern sailing. Northern ocean mariners have long known that a backing wind and a falling barometer are together a strong sign that the weather will worsen, without any specific reference to wind direction, nor to the actual value of the barometer reading. The *Wind Barometer Indications* shown in the side bar were published on every US weather map from 1904 to 1941.

By the turn of the century, however, things changed in the use of barometers at sea. Aneroid

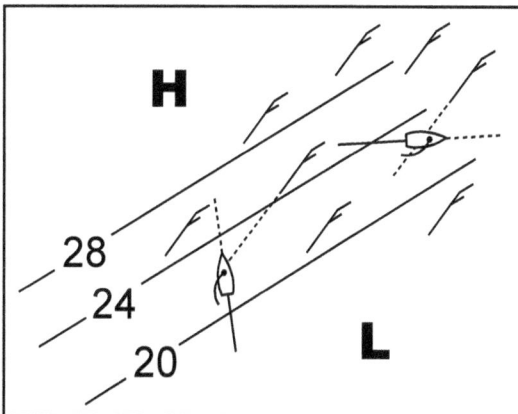

Figure 1. *North of the equator and well away from land, a starboard tack takes you into higher pressure; a port tack into lower pressure*

barometers had replaced most of the mercury instruments, which had some good consequences, and some less so. The aneroids were easier to read and maintain, and became popular quickly. Even more barometers were onboard, and were being watched and used for weather tactics. Unfortunately, it appears that with the ease of use came a lessening of the understanding of how they worked. (It is not unlike the fact that GPS caused a decline in the study of real navigation.)

The accuracy of the reading was becoming confused with the precision of the reading, and with this, the decline in real knowledge of accurate pressure began. Many of the aneroid instruments in those days were actually very good, just as a few outstanding models today, which are even better. But the importance of calibrating the instruments was not adequately appreciated.

The value of accurate pressure slipped out of the maritime meteorology training, to leave us with the still lingering view that it is only the trends and rates that matter to mariners.

So what has changed now that brings us back to using accurate pressures? There are a couple things. First we have surface weather maps now, and they get better all the time, both in analysis and in forecasts. We can use these to greatest advantage if we have accurate pressure. And we have technology now for determining accurate pressure once again—without having to resort to wieldy mercury tubes. We have modest priced electronic barometers that once set to an accurate pressure will give reliable data to within about 1 mb over the full span of typical pressures at sea.

And we also have the rediscovery of some remarkable aneroid barometers such as the Fischer Precision Aneroid Barometer, which provides pressure data to accuracies of well below 1 mb, even down into hurricane pressures. But most important of all, we have the Internet. With on-line atmospheric pressure data, live and archived, we can easily calibrate any quality barometer we have so it can be used to determine accurate pressures. There are numerous sources. A very convenient one is www.starpath.com/barometers, which finds for you the 10 closest places to your location that offers accurate pressure data, along with the range and bearing to each. It also gives the accurate elevation of your location and the

associated pressure correction, and instructions for the process.

Use of Accurate Pressure

The use of accurate pressure for tropical storm warning like the 19th century mariners did it is mentioned briefly in Bowditch. More details, and the crucial global pressure data required are given in *The Barometer Handbook*.

Outside of the tropics, the most frequent use of accurate pressure is to first confirm the surface analysis maps by comparing the mapped value with what you observed at the valid time of the map. Then, if that seems in order, we can use *target pressures* on the forecast maps to set and monitor a specific route.

The process is analogous to laying out your course line on a chart, and noticing you will be crossing over a prominent underwater shelf that should show up nicely on your depth sounder. So you mark this "target depth" as the place the depth sounder should plummet if you are on course. Then watch to see if you are right. In chart navigation and in weather routing, it is just another way to check that things are the way you think they are.

Sailing Around Highs

Most summertime transoceanic sailing routes involve going around a large mid-ocean High. The reason for going around is there is no wind in the middle of the High. The situation is shown schematically in Figure 2. You can flip, mirror, or rotate this picture for other oceans or routes.

The fundamental step is to know you must go around it, and start your route with that climatic knowledge. In other words, regardless of what the forecasts say about the wind at the location of the High when you depart, it takes too long to get there, and the map could be different by then. Statistically it is even likely to be so—meaning if you see wind there now when you are not supposed to, then chances are it will be gone when you do get there. We are looking here some 600 miles ahead, which could be 4 or 5 days away.

The usual tactical decision then is how close can you cut the corner and not run out of wind. Keys are judging the stability of the High from

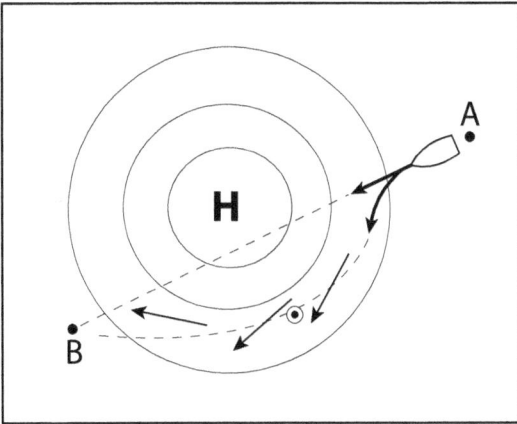

Figure 2. *Rounding a High. The circled dot shows the target pressure that should mark the peak pressure at the corner if nothing changes. You can set target pressures right on the dial of the barometer using the marker needle.*

its surface shape and location. A working rule of thumb is you will generally stay in wind if you stay 2 isobars away from the peak. If the peak value is 1030 mb, and you have a nice circular isobar at 1028, and another at 1024, then you want to stay outside of 1024. But you have to watch your barometer very closely when cut the corner. Also watch the ship reports in front of you that are plotted on the surface analysis maps. Or, with email onboard, you can send an email to

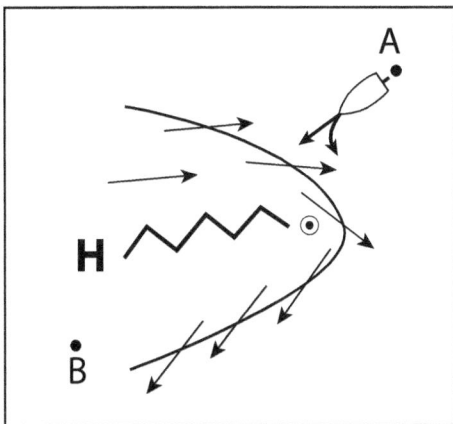

Figure 3. *This sailing route from A to B will be fastest in the following winds below the stationary ridge line. Anticipate stronger winds at the sharp bend in the isobars at the tip of the ridge. By recording a target pressure shown by the circled dot you can use your barometer to keep track of where you are relative to the ridge top. If the wind veers around and the barometer remains steady, you know you are following an isobar around the corner.*

shipreports@starpath.com with the word "help" in the subject line to learn how to get all ship reports within 300 nmi that were made during the past 6 hr. This gives wind, pressure, sea state and other data. It is also another way to check your barometer if you did not get to before leaving.

From the weather map in hand you can read the highest pressure you expect as you round the corner and set that as a target pressure to watch for. If all goes as planned, the pressure will start down again once you reach that peak. If it does not, you have to consider that the High is building, or moving toward you. If the pressure starts back down before reaching the target pressure, then the High is weakening or slipping away from you.

Crossing a Ridge

A similar choice can be confronted when approaching the top of a ridge (Figure 3). One side is down wind, the other side is to weather. When on a route across the top of it, you might have the opportunity to get from wrong side to right side, or to stay on the right side if you are already doing well. Again, due to the slow speed of a sailboat, it is not feasible to make major adjustments, but sometimes you can maneuver enough to make a difference. The forecast maps plus your dead reckoning are the only way to evaluate this.

Crossing a Trough

The best laid sailing plan around the corner of a High can still get invaded by a low pressure system where we don't want it. You are not going to maneuver around giant extratropical Lows, but you might just end up on the wrong side of a much more localized trough of low pressure. You might, for example, be headed down the east side of a near stationary trough in head winds for several days, whereas if you fell off for a while and crossed the trough you would bite the bullet for a day and then get into downwind conditions (Figure 4).

Look at the forecast maps to see if your speed and position on the alternative courses pans out with this reasoning. Watch the pressure to judge your progress. The pressure will be at a minimum as you cross the trough line. You should be able to monitor your progress with the barometer

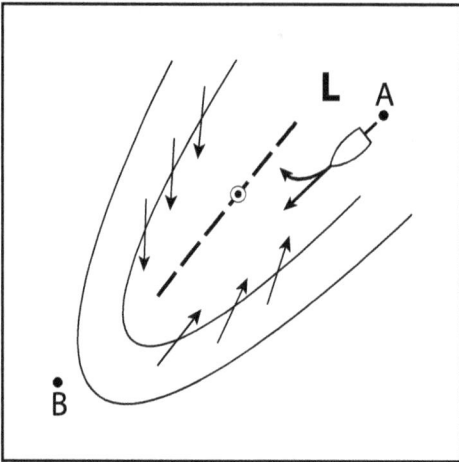

Figure 4. *The sailing route from A to B will be fastest in the following winds above the trough line. The trough line will be at local minimum in the pressure so it should be detectable underway. This maneuver would work best when the trough is moving toward you. The target pressure marking the minimum pressure expected at the trough line is shown as a circled dot.*

and know when you are across it. If the trough is sliding toward you this could be a very efficient maneuver. If it is slipping away from you, on the other hand, this might not work at all.

This same logic would apply, and maybe more often, depending on where you sail, to an approaching front, which is always a trough of low pressure, but with more significant winds and more sudden changes at the front line. §

WIND BAROMETER INDICATIONS*

When the wind sets in from points between south and southeast, and the barometer falls steadily, a storm is approaching from the west or northwest, and its center will pass near or north of the observer within 12 to 24 hours with wind shifting to northwest by way of southwest and west.

When the wind sets in from points between east and northeast and the barometer falls steadily, a storm is approaching from the south or southwest, and its center will pass near or to the south or east of the observer within 12 to 24 hours with wind shifting to northwest by way of north.

The rapidity of the storm's approach and its intensity will be indicated by the rate and the amount of the fall in the barometer.

Printed on all US weather maps from 1904 to 1941.

"4-5-6" Guideline to pressure as strong wind forecaster when present winds are fair	
Likely Significance	*Steady pressure drop over 6 Hours*
Alert	Less than 3 mb
Caution	3 to 4 mb
Definite warning	4 to 5 mb
Too late for forecasting	More than 5 mb

We proposed this rule in the mid 80s as a working guide to pressure warnings. We have had good feedback on it over the years, and have not come up with better. Such rules are never gospel. Pressure can decrease for several reasons: the low could be deepening, moving toward you, or you could be moving toward it—or any combination of the above. Nevertheless, the red flag should be up at 4-5 mb drop in a 6 hr period. Keep in mind, too, that in some systems the very strongest winds come at the back side of the storm when the pressure actually starts to rise—called "the sting in the scorpion's tail." Hence the restrictions on the 4-5-6 rule that the present winds must be fair.

ASCAT — WIND AT SEA

Granted, there are such things as fog and rain, even snow and ice, but in the end, marine weather boils down to *wind*. For sailors, wind is our engine. For all mariners, it is the wind that makes the waves, which is the ultimate threat to the progress and safety of any vessel.

We naturally think most often of the threats presented by very strong winds, but as prudent sailors, we will far more often use our knowledge of marine weather to find more wind or better wind rather than to avoid too much wind. That is why we are prudent—we do not go sailing where and when we expect strong winds.

To plan a route we need to know the wind. In coastal waters we have many observations to rely on. Some are broadcast on NOAA VHF weather (usually updated every 3 hr), but we can find even better data at the National Data Buoy Center (NDBC) online at www.ndbc.noaa.gov, updated every hour. In 3G phone range you can get the winds on a smart phone. There are apps for that — but if you use an app, check that it is right! I see some that are more than an hour late, which totally defeats the purpose. Remember you can view the latest data directly from the NDBC website and then save the link on your phone screen for later quick access. You can also get the data on a dumb phone. Use the Dial-a-Buoy service by calling 888-701-8992. When the smart phone is wrong, the dumb phone becomes smart.

Once land drops below the horizon, we need a satellite phone or SSB radio to get wind data.

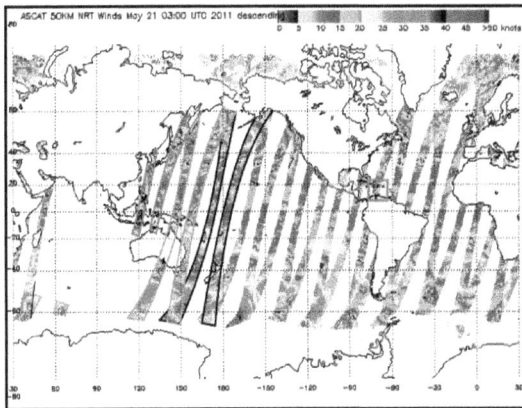

Figure 1. *Graphic index to the last 22 hours of ASCAT wind data, updated hourly from manati.orbit. nesdis.noaa.gov/datasets/ASCATData.php. Click any part of a pass to see actual data. The red box is shown in Fig. 2. The red track on the left is the most recent data, orange is 1h 41 earlier, black is another 1h 41m earlier. In the next hour the red track will be completed and then continue down across the Indian Ocean. The oldest data is the green in the bottom left corner. It will not show up in the next plot. These are the descending passes; another plot shows the ascending passes. Notice the nadir gaps of missing data that are directly under the satellite. Thus a single pass has two swaths of data.*

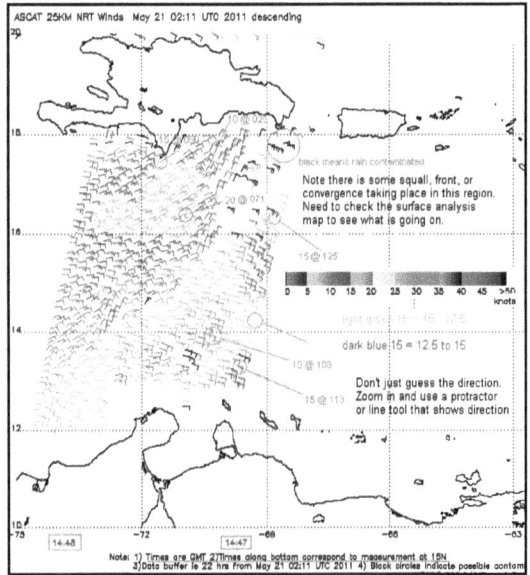

Figure 2. *Data from the red square of Fig. 1 showing color coded ocean surface winds. Black feathers mean the wind data are corrupted by rain, implying local or large scale convection. Valid times are on the bottom of the picture along with the specific latitude they apply to. It takes the satellite about 30 min to go from top to bottom of the swaths in Fig 1.*

But where would this data come from? There are a few buoys floating around that measure and report the wind, but not nearly enough to count on. What we do have is a European satellite circling the earth every 101 minutes that is recording a continuous radar image of the ocean surface in six directions, and from these data a computer analysis can determine the speed and direction of the ocean surface winds, worldwide.

As with conventional radar, the amount of microwave back scatter available to detect by radar depends on the roughness of the surface and the angle of incidence. The roughness of the sea surface depends on the strength of the wind blowing over it. Stronger winds make bigger and deeper cat's paws on the surface of the waves leading to stronger radar signals, implying stronger winds. The cat's paws are always lined up with the instantaneous direction of the true wind, unlike the waves and swells that the cat's paws are riding on, whose direction may differ from the true wind direction.

Needless to say, a complex scientific analysis is required to extract wind data from the radar data, but it is much aided by empirical results. In other words, the satellite can measure the radar backscattering near buoys that have known winds, and then the analysis can be adjusted to match these known values, and then these adjustments can be applied to cases without buoy data.

The satellite name is Metop-A. The instrument it carries that is doing the job is called the Advanced Scatterometer, or ASCAT. It is operated by the European Organization for the Exploitation of Meteorological Satellites (www.eumetsat. int). Available data are analyzed by several organizations, notable ones being the Royal Netherlands Meteorological Institute (www.knmi. nl/scatterometer) and the Ocean Surface Winds Team (OSWT) of the Center for Satellite Application and Research, a division of NOAA (manati. orbit.nesdis.noaa.gov/datasets/ASCATData.php).

Although ASCAT has been operational since 2007 and the data have been available to US meteorologists since 2009, it is only more recently become available to the public. Mariners so far have only limited access via graphic images of the wind fields, but hopefully in the near future we will have access to digital vector data as we once had with the American QuikSCAT satellite and its SeaWinds scatterometer. That instrument failed in late 2009 after a much longer than expected lifetime of tremendous service to meteorological science. QuikSCAT winds were available to mariners via GRIB files, which is a format very popular with ocean going sailors.

In a sense, QuikSCAT came and went like Loran-C did. It was gone before the majority of mariners knew the nuances of using it to its full potential. ASCAT promises to be more enduring

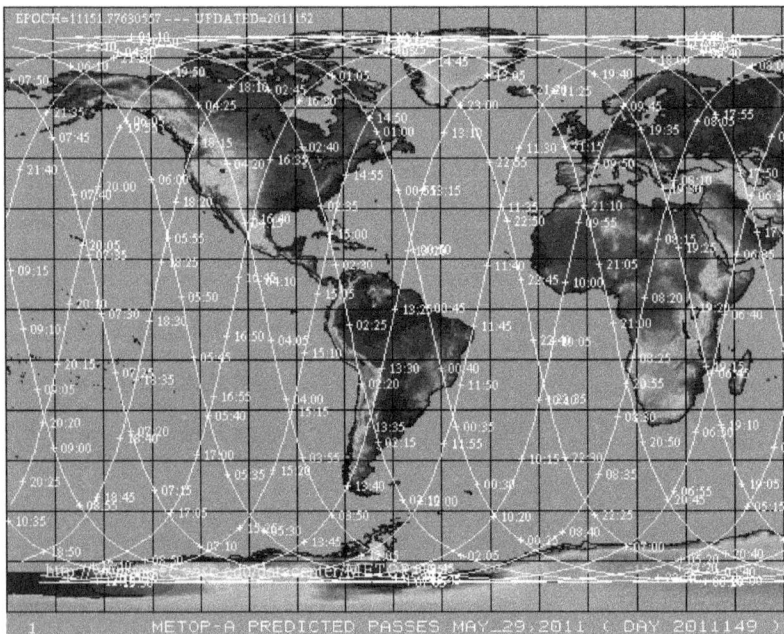

Figure 3. *One way to predict when ASCAT data will become available. Check this plot from www.ssec.wisc.edu/ datacenter/METOP-A, find the time of closest passage (keeping in mind the nadir gap), add 2h and 30m to that time, then round up to the next whole hour and that will be the UTC of next available data at the website listed in Fig. 1. You may get data a bit earlier than that or a bit later if your corrected time is near a whole hour time, but that is our working guideline.*

in that it is funded for at least two more satellite lifetimes. QuikSCAT was a onetime program, but we have very much to thank for it, not the least of which is the wonderful Climatology of Global Ocean Winds (COGOW) program (cioss.coas.oregonstate.edu/cogow), which is now the state of the art global winds atlas that replaces all earlier work, including US and British pilot chart wind data. We also owe the now commonly used wind category "hurricane force winds" to studies of extratropical storms using QuikSCAT data. These studies revealed that more than expected high latitude storms had winds higher than 64 kts, and thus the value of the new descriptor.

To view the latest ASCAT data, go to the OSWT website where you find a graphic index to the latest 22 hours of satellite passes. Then click a region of interest to see the wind fields. Wind speeds are color coded, and with little practice values can be read to within a few knots. The earth rotates beneath Metop-A's low earth polar orbit, so each plot on earth of the satellite track in the same direction is tilted to the west and shifted by about 25° of longitude. The valid times of each pass are listed in small print at the bottom of each page of the zoomed selections. Each pass will be 101 minutes (1 hr 41min) apart. The two directions, ascending and descending tracks, are presented in separate plots so the data do not get confused.

The first thing we learn from this data is that, unlike QuikSCAT, the ASCAT data has a large gap of missing data along the sub-satellite track, called the nadir gap. This comes about because of the type of scatterometer used, which is a differ-

ent design from what QuikSCAT used. QuikSCAT did not have this gap. This is definitely a handicap to work around, as we do not get as full a picture of the wind pattern. But we are getting near real time ocean winds and all such information is helpful. Remember, these are observations; they are not forecasts or interpolations from isobars. The latest data are between 2 and 3 hours old.

These wind data are not only what we need to confirm the latest weather map and plan a route, they are also exactly what the NWS needs for their numerical weather models such as the Global Forecast System (GFS). The ASCAT observed wind field implies the lay of the true isobars, which is one of the main surface results of the models. When we download a GRIB wind field to the boat from one of the various commercial suppliers, they are giving us the GFS model predictions of the winds—some services offer other numerical models as well. The quality of these predictions depends in large part on the quality of the wind and pressure observations that seed the computations.

The ASCAT wind data have been assimilated into the GFS model since May, 2011. This means when we compare ASCAT winds at a synoptic time (00, 06, 12, 18 UTC) with the corresponding initial wind map from a GRIB download, these two ought to agree fairly well. In this case the GFS winds are pretty much forced to match the ASCAT winds. Recall that the initial map of any GRIB download is essentially a surface analysis at a synoptic time, but subsequent ones are forecasts.

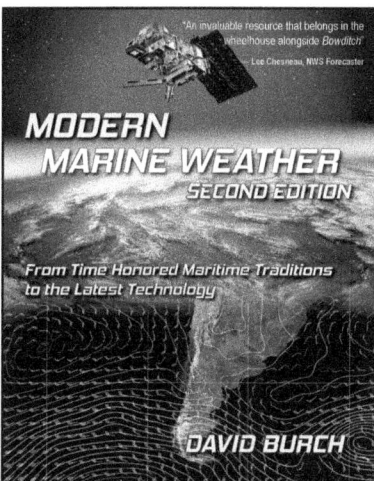

Figure 4. *This textbook explains how to use scatterometer wind data such as ASCAT for weather analysis and route planning. The examples use QuikSCAT data, as well as the new ASCAT and OSCAT, but the source is not crucial to understanding the many diverse and important applications of the results. The book is available worldwide in print or ebook format. We do not know of any other book that covers this topic.*

If the area you care about most has ASCAT data at the nearest synoptic time, then chances are you get a better than average forecast. Other times these resources may not coincide in time or space, and then we have to use them separately. For example, if we need to choose where to cross the doldrums, we can look at the model predictions for best location, and then check the closest place in space and time between model forecast and ASCAT observations. If there is a difference, remember the ASCAT winds are real data; the GRIBs are predictions. When the times coincide, we can see remarkable detail in the initial GRIB wind map as shown in the illustration.

The ASCAT data can be especially valuable, ie gold-like, for ocean sailors trying to figure how close they can cut the corner of a mid-ocean High. Instead of relying on the raw fate of a computer model and an isolated ship report or two, you can now look at actual winds on the edge of the High.

As of this printing, the only way we know of to get ASCAT data underway (short of a satellite internet connection) is through a free email service set up by Starpath. It will provide you with the graphic images of the latest wind fields for the lat and lon you request. For details see www.starpath.com/ascat, which also includes news and updates on this important source of marine weather data and related articles on tactical use of the data. There is now, for example, a new source of scatterometer data from India, called OSCAT. This is also very good data, and the swath widths are large, without a nadir gap, just like the QuikSCAT was.

Nuances in the use and interpretation of the scatterometer wind data are covered in the book *Modern Marine Weather, 2nd edition.*

One such interesting nuance is that now Metop-B, the second generation of this satellite, is now operative and following along the same track as Metop-A, but preceeding it by 45 min. The wind analysis is identical on both, so if the wind pattern is stable we expect to see the identical wind in both passes. But when there are squalls or rapidly changing winds, you can actually see this differences in the two passes, just 45 minutes apart. We have set up a web page for tropical Altantic weather where we compare the two passes side by side. You can make similar comparisons for any part of the world. See www.starpath.com/oarnw. §

Navigation in Hurricane Season

The tragic sinking of the tall ship Bounty and the loss of two lives on Monday, Oct 28, 2012 in the winds and seas of a very well forecasted storm forces me to postpone the promised article on pros and cons of echart types, and instead go over the guidelines we have for safe navigation in the presence of tropical storms. But first an acknowledgement that all mariners are grateful to the courage and skill of the USCG team who risked their own lives to rescue the 14 crew members of the Bounty who were at the site when the helicopter got there.

In *Modern Marine Weather* we point out that if you want to sail in a hurricane you can. We know where they take place and when they take place—and when they do occur, their location and projected tracks are remarkably well forecasted. To sail in one, just look up this information and go there. On the other hand, if you do not want to

sail in a hurricane, look up the same information and then do not go there.

Seems simple enough, but this nutshell summary of avoiding hurricanes is obviously over-simplified. Huge areas of the ocean and long seasons would be blocked out by such a simple guideline. Fortunately, the National Hurricane Center (NHC), in collaboration with experienced mariners over the years, has come up with more realistic guidelines for safe navigation in the presence of tropical systems. It comes in the form of two simple rules: The 34-kt Rule and The Mariner's 1-2-3 Rule.

The 1-2-3 Rule is simple and easy to apply based on text or voice reports of the storm locations, which are given several times a day in the high-seas broadcasts. Namely, the danger area to be avoided expands the forecasted danger zone by 100 nmi per day, as shown in Figure 1.

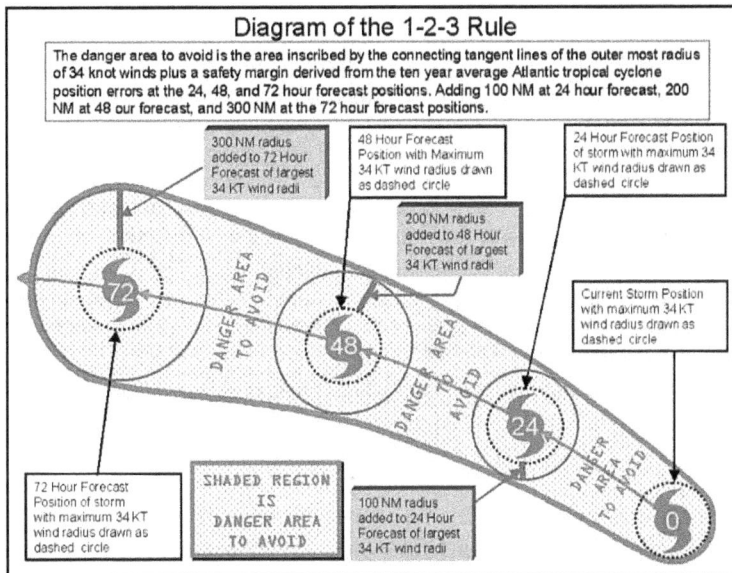

Figure 1. *The 34-kt Rule: "For vessels at sea, avoiding the 34-kt wind field of a hurricane is paramount." The Mariner's 1-2-3 Rule: Add a safety margin to the 34-kt Rule of 100 nmi for each day into the forecast. The 34-kt radii are given in the text or voice broadcasts for each quadrant of the storm (see sidebar). There are also 50-kt wind radii given in the forecasts, but these are not used in the Rules being discussed.*

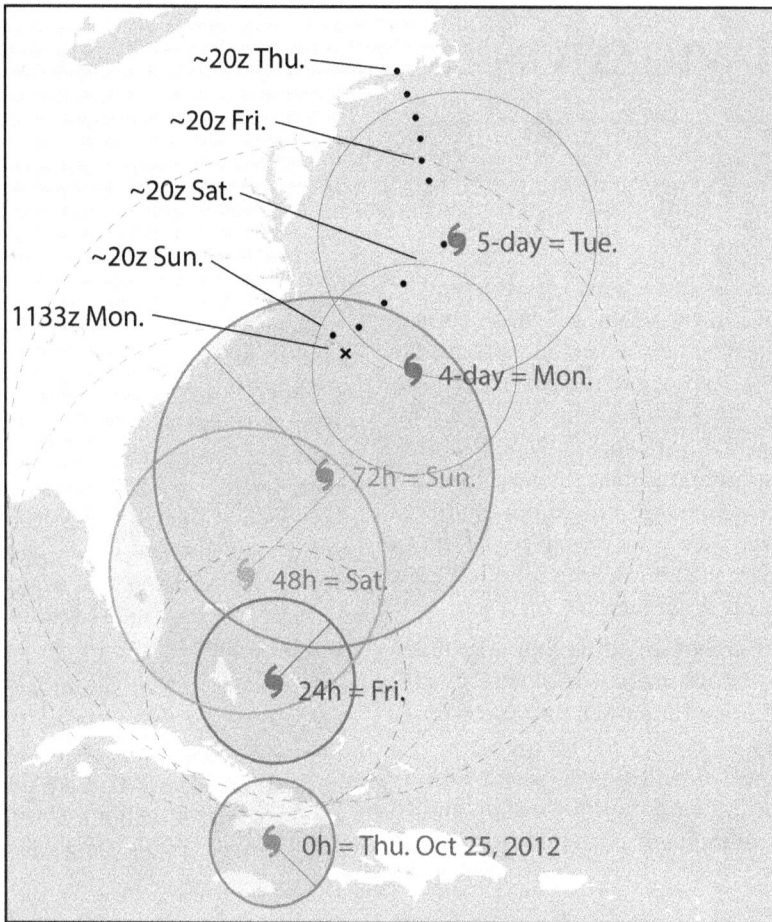

Figure 2. *Plot of the 3-day and extended forecasts for Hurricane Sandy issued on Thursday, Oct 25, 2012, valid at 00z. Also shown is the track of the HMS Bounty which departed for Florida on that date. The shaded areas encompass the 34-kt wind regions for the next three days, with the radial lines marked that showed the largest radius in each case. The associated colored dashed circles mark the limits of the Mariners 1-2-3 Rule. The two top storm locations mark the extended forecasts, with the dark circles marking the quoted uncertainties in track location. These two dark circles do not imply any wind or storm size predictions. The 5-day forecast of the ECMRF model called correctly for an earlier turn to the west than the GFS model did, but the NHC always balances the input from multiple models when making their forecasts.*

In this storm, it was well forecasted that the hurricane would turn extratropical, expand, and intensify, so the 34-kt Rule alone blocked off essentially all of the coastal waters before even applying the 1-2-3 Rule. The 1-2-3 Rule showed how far out to sea the risk extended and remained a valuable guide to mariners in the waters off Florida for several days. Figure 3 shows this extra caution was justified.

The diagram shows the forecast at the time of departure. The inevitability of the encounter with the 34-kt wind field did not diminish with time.

The danger zone for this application is characterized by the NHC as the radius about the storm center that includes winds greater than 34 kt. Thus we start with what the NHC calls The 34-kt Rule: "For vessels at sea, avoiding the 34-kt wind field of a hurricane is paramount. Thirty-four knots is chosen as the critical value because as wind speed increases to this speed, sea state development approaches critical levels resulting in rapidly decreasing limits to ship maneuverability." They add the natural precaution that sea state outside of the 34-kt radius can also be significant enough to limit course and speed options, so we should monitor this carefully.

We can use the forecast of Hurricane Sandy on Thursday, Oct 25 (sidebar) as an example of a long-term forecast for a storm headed north.

Plot the location of the storm at forecast time, and then plot on your chart the forecasted locations on day 1, 2, and 3. Then check the forecast for the maximum radius of 34-kt winds. They are given for each quadrant on each day's forecast. On Day 1 this was 150 nmi, which occurred in the NE quadrant. With a drawing compass draw a circle around each of the 3 locations with 34-kt radii (in this example) of 150, 250, and 300 nmi. You then have a plot of forecasted storm sizes on these 3 days, which is shown in Figure 2.

These are not the safety zones of the 1-2-3 Rule, these are the actual forecasted locations and sizes of the system that should be avoided. Next we apply the Mariner's 1-2-3 Rule to account for uncertainties in forecast accuracy.

To each of these 3 radii, we then add 100, 200, and 300 nmi to account for historic uncertainty in the forecasted track. This guideline is based on the NHC's records over the past 10 years of past errors in forecast track location. The track locations are actually more precise than this in recent years, and indeed getting better continually, but the uncertainty in intensity and size of the forecasted systems remains more of a challenge and hence the larger safety zones.

Furthermore, this guideline as presented is for tropical systems that are fueled from the warm water below them. Once a storm moves out of the tropics and becomes extratropical, it begins to gain energy from a much broader source—the temperature difference between cool northern air and warmer southern air masses. When this happens the system can quickly become much larger and more intense. This is precisely what happened with the transition between Hurricane Sandy and "Superstorm Sandy." It got much larger, with a much broader band of strong winds and high seas.

This one became known in the media as a "superstorm" (not a defined meteorological term) because that transition took place at a time that was uniquely favorable to enhanced extratropical development. Extratropical storms on the surface are strongly influenced by the wind patterns in the upper atmosphere, and this one just hap-

---

NWS NATIONAL HURRICANE CENTER MIAMI FL

0300 UTC THU OCT 25 2012

[Day 0 - Thursday]

HURRICANE CENTER LOCATED NEAR 19.4N 76.3W AT 25/0300Z. POSITION ACCURATE WITHIN 20 NM PRESENT MOVEMENT TOWARD THE NORTH OR 10 DEGREES AT 11 KT. ESTIMATED MINIMUM CENTRAL PRESSURE 954 MB. EYE DIAMETER 20 NM. MAX SUSTAINED WINDS 80 KT WITH GUSTS TO 100 KT.

64 KT....... 25NE 20SE 20SW 20NW. 50 KT....... 50NE 60SE 40SW 40NW. 34 KT.......110NE 120SE 70SW 60NW. 12 FT SEAS..120NE 300SE 120SW 120NW. WINDS AND SEAS VARY GREATLY IN EACH QUADRANT. RADII IN NAUTICAL MILES ARE THE LARGEST RADII EXPECTED ANYWHERE IN THAT QUADRANT.

[Day 1 Friday]

FORECAST VALID 26/0000Z 24.4N 76.2W MAX WIND 70 KT...GUSTS 85 KT. 64 KT... 20NE 20SE 0SW 0NW. 50 KT... 70NE 70SE 40SW 50NW. 34 KT...150NE 120SE 70SW 90NW.

[Day 2 Saturday]

FORECAST VALID 27/0000Z 27.6N 77.2W MAX WIND 65 KT...GUSTS 80 KT. 50 KT...120NE 100SE 90SW 120NW. 34 KT...250NE 160SE 100SW 230NW.

[Day 3 Sunday]

FORECAST VALID 28/0000Z 30.5N 74.5W MAX WIND 60 KT...GUSTS 75 KT. 50 KT...120NE 120SE 120SW 100NW. 34 KT...300NE 270SE 180SW 300NW.

EXTENDED OUTLOOK. NOTE...ERRORS FOR TRACK HAVE AVERAGED NEAR 175 NM ON DAY 4 AND 225 NM ON DAY 5... AND FOR INTENSITY NEAR 20 KT EACH DAY.

[Day 4 Monday]

OUTLOOK VALID 29/0000Z 33.5N 71.5W MAX WIND 60 KT...GUSTS 75 KT.

[Day 5 Tuesday]

OUTLOOK VALID 30/0000Z 37.0N 70.0W... POSTTROPICAL MAX WIND 60 KT...GUSTS 75 KT.

pened to move north at the worst possible time—not only for enhancement, but for a forced turn to the west, rather than the more normal route to the east. This, however, was not a surprise. This storm was indeed a testimony to the skill of modern numerical weather prediction, which had ac-counted for these effects. They were included in the forecasts as shown by the examples here.

In short, we should not look at The 34-kt Rule and The Mariner's 1-2-3 Rule as an over-conserva-tive guideline. It was spot on in the case of Sandy, with tragic consequences for the Bounty. §

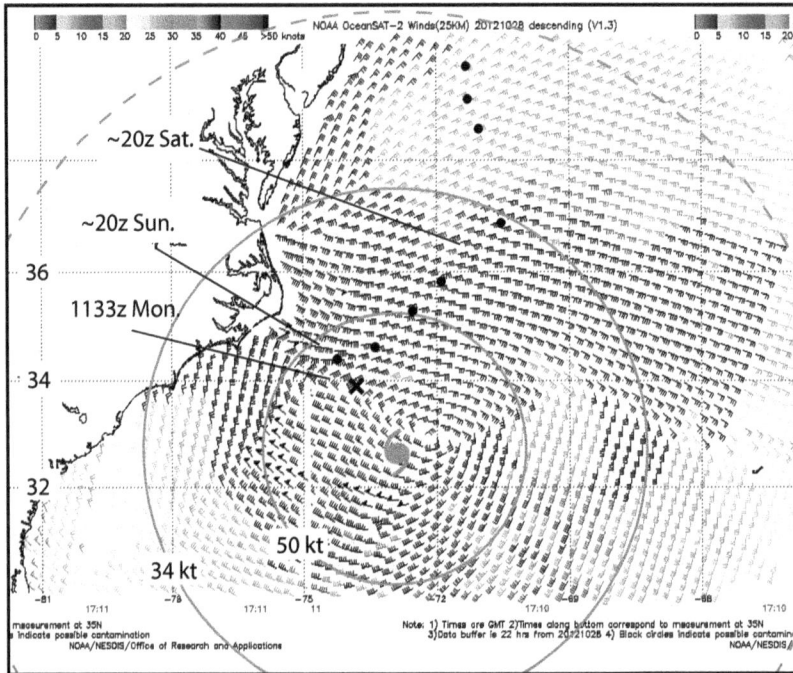

Figure 3. *Satellite wind measurements at 1710z on Sunday, Oct 28, 2012. For comparison, the 72-hr fore-casted location of the storm for that time made four days earlier on Thursday is shown, along with the 34-kt wind and 50-kt wind radii. (Color data online and in the ebook version helps interpret the wind speeds.)*

The 50-kt wind field was very well forecasted, and for the most part the 34-kt winds as well. But there were large regions of the ocean beyond that 34-kt radius that had winds well above 34-kt, which shows the value of the 1-2-3 Rule. That rule at 72 hr off calls for a large clearance in such a large storm. For storms within the tropics the 34-kt wind range might not be as large, so maneuvering options could be better, but tropical storm sizes do vary significantly within the tropics.

The NHC website publishes the 1-2-3 Rule boundaries for all storms they track, so watching these online is a good way to get a feeling for how they evolve.

The satellite data here are from the Indian scatterometer OceanSat2 (OSCAT). The European instrument ASCAT is a primary source for this type of data, but it did not have a pass at this time. The sections it did show confirm that the winds were at least as strong as shown here. We have made a link to all of the scat-terometer data along with a convenient way to get ASCAT winds by email at www. starpath.com/ascat.

For further information see:

www.nhc.noaa.gov/prepare/marine.php

www.starpath.com/ascat

www.nhc.noaa.gov/marine

www.ecmwf.int

www.starpath.com/weatherbook

PREDICTING FOG

One morning a few weeks ago, we were overlooking a foggy Puget Sound planning a cruise to the San Juans for the next day. For the past few days we had had the same weather pattern—fog at daybreak, burning off sometime in the morning. But it was already noon and still just half a mile visibility. The local VHF marine weather forecast was no help. Strangely enough it did not mention fog at all. So the challenge we address here is how do we predict on our own when such a fog will lift, and what is likely to happen the following day? (We can guess right now that fog formation is somehow the opposite of fog dissipating, so if we can predict one, we can likely predict the other.)

The fog being experienced in this example comes about when we have a moist air mass over us in a relatively high pressure. High pressure means clear skies, and without cloud cover to keep us warm after the sun goes down (greenhouse effect), the surface air cools rapidly as the surface heat radiates away at night. A drop of 15 to 20° F is not uncommon in these conditions. When the air temperature drops to the dew point, water vapor in the air condenses into fog. It will remain foggy until the temperature rises above the dew point. This is called radiation fog. It generally forms on land and spills down onto the water.

It is a mystery why the marine forecasts did not discuss the fog in that example—had they discussed it, however, we likely would not be discussing it now. It could be the automated light beam that measures the visibility was not working, or its path happened to be located in a pocket of clear air. Obviously no one contributing to those reports could see Puget Sound. Normally fog predictions are exceptionally good, even when wind predictions are very wrong. In a moment we see exactly how anyone could know exactly when this was going to lift and also when it might form again.

Air temperature and dew point are air mass properties that are uniform over large areas and easy to measure and forecast. Wind over a wide mountain valley like Puget Sound, on the other hand, can change dramatically with a few degrees rotation of the isobars. It is not uncommon in this area to get a wind forecast of "variable 5 to 15." Variable means the wind direction is unknown; "5 to 15" is another way to say "0 to 15," which means the wind speed is also unknown. The same broadcast could then forecast afternoon temperatures and dew points accurate to 1° out of 60 or so, and they would most likely be right. So we can predict the behavior of fog as soon as we find access to these accurate predictions for air temperature and dew point.

But I should stress once again, even though we are now fog sleuthing on our own, normally maritime fog or reduced visibility prediction is very accurate and dependable when it is reported. What we are about to do just fine tunes reports that might exist, and also fine tune other observations, such as what hour of the day we expect a front to cross our waterway with a sudden change in wind. This type of detail is never in the radio broadcasts, but is readily available to us by other means. That is not to say such fine details will be right all the time, but they are at least letting us see what the best science on the subject has to offer.

This exercise might also serve as an introduction to one of the very best marine weather sources on the Internet, but one that is only slowly being discovered by sailors, even though it has been right in front of us for about a year or so. The trouble with finding it online is the word "weather" (even "marine weather") is a complete disaster in any Internet search engine. It might be reassuring to know that the best source is the National Weather Service (NWS) themselves, but this does not help us find it. Commercial services, which rarely add to the NWS content, manage to

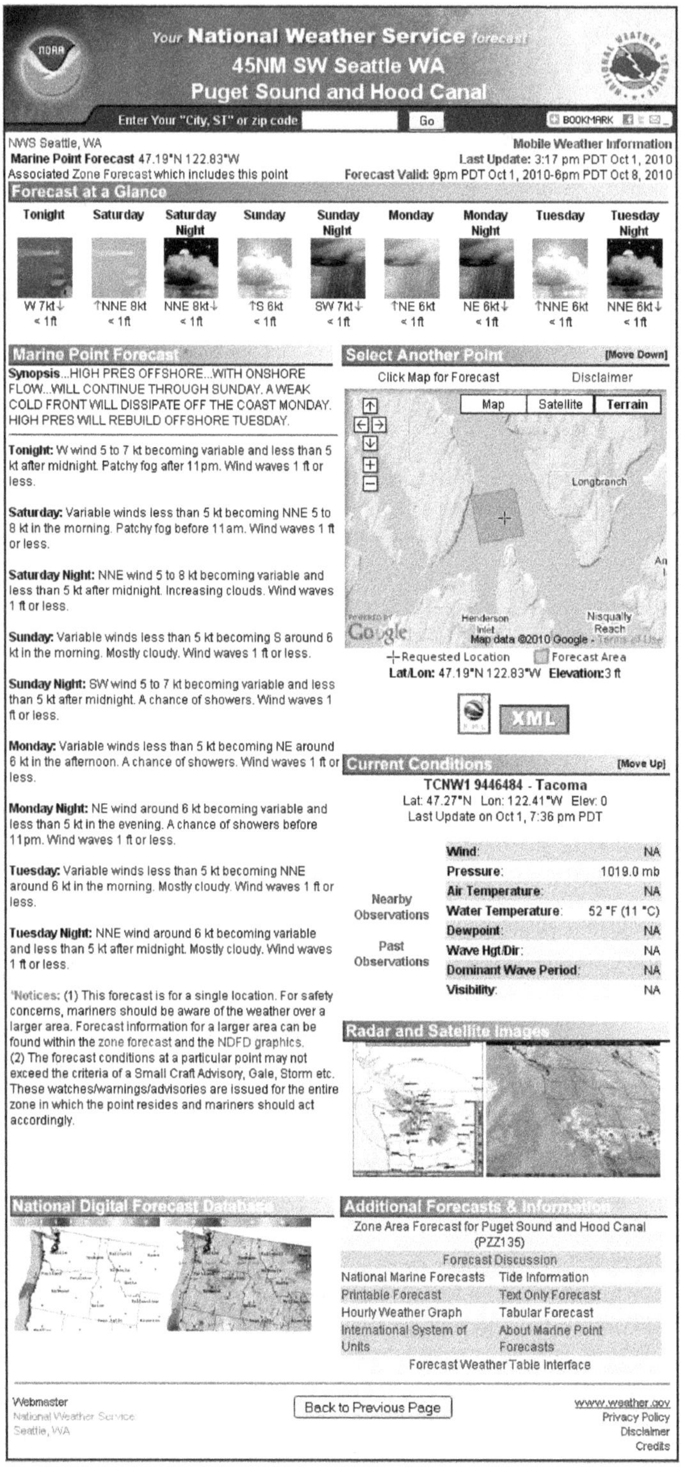

Figure 1. *Clicking the interactive map gives land weather for land clicks and marine weather for water clicks. Then click the bottom right link called Hourly Weather Graph for timing details.*

grab all the weather traffic. So here is a step by step route to the NWS data.

(1) Go to this link: http://forecast.weather.gov/zipcity.php.

(If for any reason that link stops working, go to www.starpath.com/navpubs for an updated link. There are other things of interest to navigators there as well.)

(2) Enter city, state, or zip of the nearest town to the waterway of interest. You will then get to the page that is used for land based weather, an example of which is shown in Figure 1. This is the same page you might bookmark for deciding what clothes to wear to work, or whether it will rain on an event you care about. This is the "secret source" we are looking for!

(3) Now drag and zoom the inset map so that you see clearly the waterway you care about. You can actually open this page for New York City, then zoom way out, drag to Florida, and zoom back in to get weather for Key West waters. It does not matter how you get to this page with this interactive inset map.

(4) Once you have your waterway in view, double click the water at that location. It is important that you click water and not land. You should see a small red square show up that marks the region of your forecast on the inset map. The page will now have magically switched from land weather to marine weather. You triggered this by clicking water rather than land. Again, you may want to bookmark this location, which gives all of the standard marine weather information we get various places. The special information is in the next step.

(5) Now scroll to the bottom of the page to find a link on the right called: Hourly Weather Graph and click that link. Then uncheck all data boxes except Temperature, Dew Point, and Surface Wind (kt), and click Submit. You will see a display like that of Figure 2. Later you might want to look at the detailed sea state forecasts, but for now we concentrate on fog. This is the picture that tells you when the air temperature will fall to the dew point and then when it is predicted to rise above it, marking the formation and dissipation of fog for that region.

To learn more as you study this process, watch the live data very closely from the nearest light house or reporting buoy (www.ndbc.noaa.gov) as you visually watch the range of visibility on the waterway. You will notice correlations between visibility and the difference between the two temperatures, even down to the fraction of a degree in some cases.

Keep in mind that you can actually view this data (hourly graphs and live reports) from a smart phone underway on many coastal and inland waters, just as you can see the weather radar

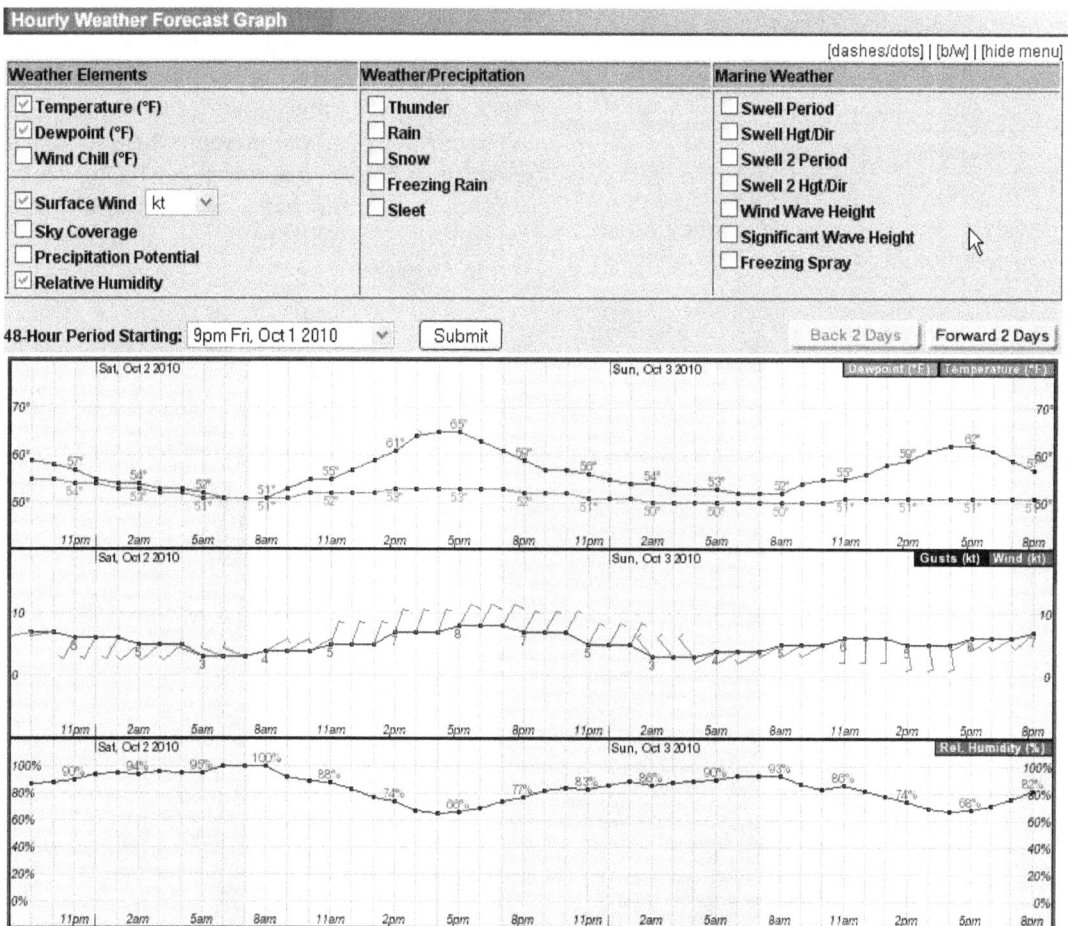

Figure 2. *When the air temperature drops to within 1° or so of the dew point we can expect fog to occur. For radiation fog, this occurs most often when the wind is light and the pressure is high. On Sat, we expect fog after about midnight and then clearing again by 9am. This data does not call for any fog the next night. Relative humidity does not help with this prediction. It is more a measure of comfort than of navigational value. Notice that the light westerly switches to a light easterly within an hour of sunrise. These sudden wind changes are usually more interesting when the wind is stronger, but when racing it matters always. Click anywhere on this graphic plot and you will get a table of the numerical values for each hour.*

images underway that show precisely where rain might be located and how it is moving.

Wind shifts at a frontal passage are always a sharp veer (shift to the right), so by looking at these same hourly graphs you can predict when a front will cross. If you are racing and expect from this data that a front will cross during your time going to weather, it will pay to be on the right hand side of the course, and so on. To my knowledge, this is the only place we have such detailed information, so readily available.

To practice using this data for wind or fog predictions, check a weather map from the Ocean Prediction Center (www.opc.ncep.noaa.gov) to find a region with a nice High in place to look for fog, or another one with a front about to pass in a day or so. Then go to that region with this weather source to see what you can learn about the timing of fog and wind.

The technology at hand these days is quite remarkable. You can even call a buoy to ask for its present weather and sometimes sea state. Call 888-701-8992 and enter station number 28963 (BUZM3, Buzzards Bay, MA) for a sample. See www.ndbc.noaa.gov/dial.shtml for details and list of station numbers. Not all stations give the dew point.

For completeness it must be said loud and clear that there is another kind of fog, called sea fog, and it does not behave this way at all. The resource we have discussed will not help in the detailed timing of sea fog episodes, but the general forecasting of them should be very good. Sea fog is formed at sea and moves around with the prevailing wind. Radiation fog is limited to light air, sea fog is not. Radiation fog has trouble developing in winds over 10, because the air is not still enough to cool down and it mixes with other layers. Some 3 to 5 kts of wind is most favorable for radiation fog formation. It lets the fog form then moves it on to pile up somewhere. Less than 3 kts or so leads to waist deep patchy fog. Dense sea fog, on the other hand, can coexist with 30 kts of wind, just as well as with calm air. It is another topic altogether. §

Figure 3. *Radiation fog spilling off of Whidbey Island into the Eastern Strait of Juan de Fuca. Aerial photo by the author.*

THE CORNER EFFECT

There is much mystery to the way wind interacts with land. We can study marine weather and become quite expert at weather routing on the open water, only to be completely humbled once we sail out into our own local waters to discover that many of the basic principles we learned no longer work. We look at one example here, and what we might do to anticipate it.

Wind flows from High to Low pressure, and then the Coriolis effect bends it to the right (in the Northern Hemeisphere). For surface winds, the main thing resisting this change in direction is the frictional drag caused by the surface itself.

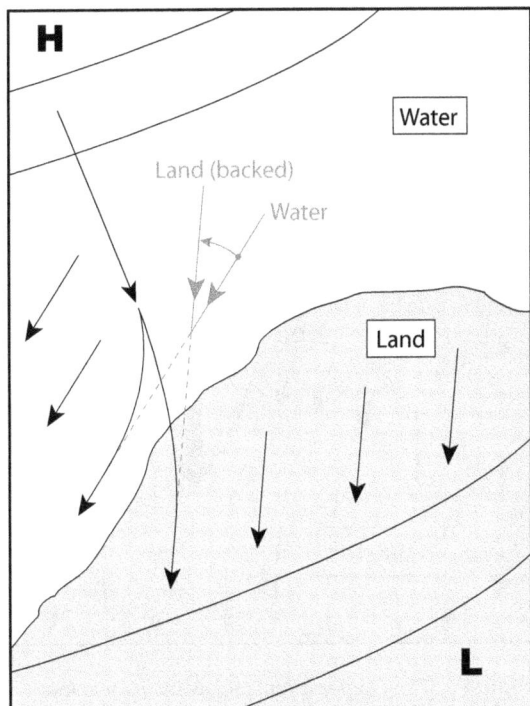

Figure 1. *When wind flows from High to Low pressure (schematic isobars shown), and then the Coriolis force bends it to the right. The higher surface friction over land prevents the wind over land from bending to the right as much as it does over water, leaving the wind on land backed relative to wind on adjacent water.*

The larger the friction, the less the wind bends. Wind flow over water has notably less friction acting on it than when the same wind blows over land. Thus we expect the wind direction to change somewhat when it crosses from water to land or vice versa—assuming of course that the wind can flow smoothly from the water to the land.

If there is a cliff or hill at the shoreline, the surface wind gets changed by other factors. Wind blowing right onto the face of a steep cliff would tend to lift to go over the cliff some distance off the cliff, sometimes giving lighter air right at the cliff face. Kayakers can sometimes take advantage of this lighter air at a leeward cliff face in some circumstances, but it would not be very good sailboat tactics to look for this kind of shelter. Indeed, if the wind is not directly onto the face of the cliff, but diagonally angled toward it, then much of the wind will most likely just turn at the cliff face and follow it along the cliff, maybe even stronger than away from the cliff.

Likewise, if the shore is not a cliff but just a large sloping hill, the wind tends to ride up over the hill without much predictability to its behavior. We can only know that there could in principle be a change, and then use binoculars on other boats, flags, and smoke stacks to try to guess what is going on. If you are tacking to get down the water way and see a boat reaching down the beach on one tack, then you learn something, even if you don't have a model for the effect.

So we are not talking now about hills or cliffs, but instead a low, flat shoreline, over which we might expect the wind to flow, more or less unobstructed, and it is this seemingly innocuous circumstance that can produce surprises.

Some standard wind terminology is crucial for the discussion. When the wind shifts to the right it is said to veer. When it shifts to the left it is said to back. A west wind that shifts to the W-NW has veered; if it shifts to the W-SW it has backed.

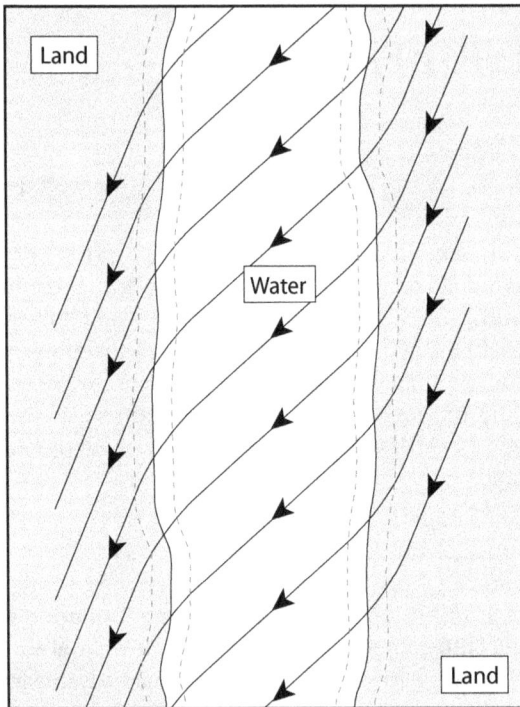

Figure 2. *Wind direction is backed over land relative to over the adjacent water. The transition between the two directions takes place in a narrow region along the shoreline.*

The definition is global and independent of wind direction. Thus wind over land that has bent less to the right is backed relative to wind over water that has bent more to the right. Once these basic terms are second nature, we can simply register in our minds that wind over land is always backed relative to wind over adjacent water, and we can expect that type of shift whenever wind crosses a low flat shoreline.

Another important point is wind shifts at a shoreline do not take place in a quantum step right at the shoreline, but rather make a smooth curving transition that spans a region on both sides of the shoreline.

The consequence of this on a point of land or corner of an island is called the Corner Effect. It is interesting because its effect on us depends on which way the wind is blowing, and whether we are going upwind or downwind. Its effect will always be opposite for points of land on opposite sides of the boat. For years we have tried to come up with some diagram or jingle that helps us re-

member what is what. The illustration shown is our best effort to date for a shorthand reminder.

When wind blows over or off the point of land it is backed relative to the wind over the water. If that backing shift is directing this land wind out onto the water, then it is converging with the water wind and that enhances the wind speed on the water near that point. On the other hand, if the backed wind direction is away from the water wind direction, then the wind in the region of the point is diverging, leading to lighter

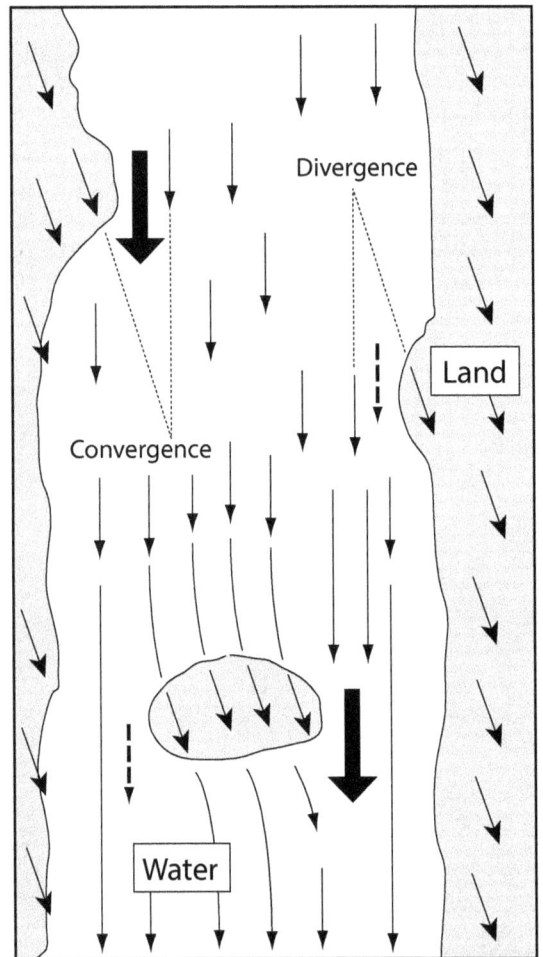

Figure 3. *The Corner Effect on low points and low islands. Where the wind flow over a low point or corner converges with the main flow of wind on the water there is an enhanced wind speed in the vicinity of the point. Likewise, when the wind diverges at the point, the wind in the region is diminished. Think of the wind coming off the land as backed relative to the main flow to decide which side has the convergence.*

air at the point. Thus in the same wind with two similar points of land on either sides of the boat you will have stronger than average wind on one point and weaker than average on the other. The effect can be anywhere from modest to dramatic, depending on the geometry and the wind. Cases we have seen where the effect is prominent were rather localized. The strong air does not extent far beyond the point, but it can be just long enough and strong enough for a nice round up.

Needless to say, the shapes and textures of points and island corners are many and diverse, and other factors mentioned and many not mentioned can enhance or diminish convergence and divergence. This may well be a way to understand behavior you have seen before—or it could be a way to explain why something did not happen that you predicted would happen. It is always good to have some of that preparation if you are the one calling the shots.

If you know of local examples that are candidates for this effect, please post them on the StarpathNav Facebook page with your experiences.

If the wind does not flow *over the corner* of low land to create a corner effect, but instead flows smoothly *around the corner* of a steeper point or island corner, you might have the opportunity to take advantage of another interaction of wind and terrain illustrated in Figure 4. It is another nice effect to look for and then repeat if it works out for you. §

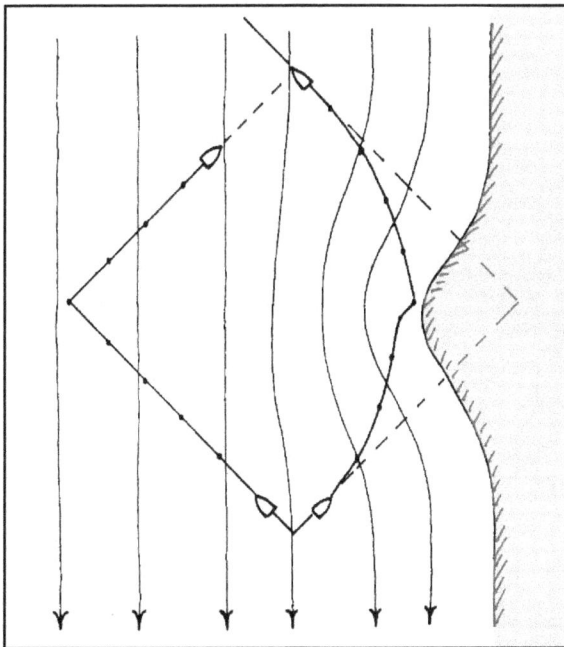

Figure 4. *The advantage of tacking at a headland when the wind follows it around the bend. Two boats start off at the bottom on opposite tacks but sailing at the same speed. The one headed to the point is continually lifted going in, and then with a judicious tack at the point is lifted on the way back out, to gain considerably on the boat staying in unperturbed air.*

OCEAN & TIDAL CURRENTS

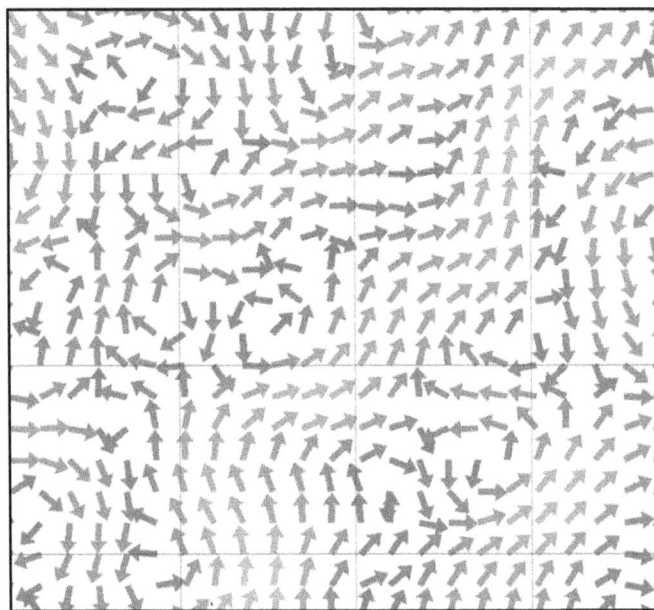

ESTIMATING AND CORRECTING FOR CURRENT SET

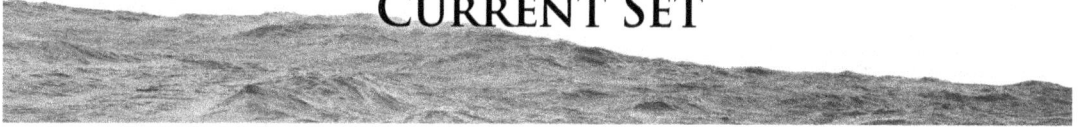

The problem with sailing in current is the boat is not moving in the direction it is headed. This is serious problem for navigation, especially at night or in the fog. The normal way to navigate in current is to define a route leg to the next waypoint from the previous one in your GPS, and head off in that direction. Then watch your zoomed in track on an electronic charting system (ECS) display to see if you are staying on that line or not. You can also tell this from the cross track error (XTE) or by comparing the COG (course over ground) output to your desired course heading. In the Jan issue we discussed using these electronic tools for navigating in these conditions, along with the several effects that might lead to your COG being different from the course you are steering.

In many cases with these electronics all working properly, we really do not need to know anything about the currents ahead of time to navigate safely and efficiently through them. Nevertheless, a navigator is always better off knowing as much about the planned route as possible, so predicating wind and current along any route is usually valuable. When your craft has limited power in areas with strong currents, however, the predictions become crucial; you might not be able to go where you want to if the route and timing are not planned properly. Sailing in Florida and other places with little tidal flow this is not often an issue, but in places like the Pacific Northwest and counterparts in Northeast waters it is. Currents of 2 to 4 kts over large areas are easy to find, and some narrow passes exceed 10 kts routinely.

For now we consider cases where currents can matter and when we might not have all these powerful tools at hand, but still need to navigate through moving water. It could be tidal currents changing every few hours, or ocean currents that are steady for days. In some cases you might have all the equipment onboard, but you are making decisions on deck without access to it. Or you could be looking at your COG which is notably different from your actual heading, and you wish to estimate what sort of current speed and direction might account for this.

The two basic questions are: what will happen to me if I do not make any adjustment for the current, and what adjustments can I make to compensate for the current so I end up where I want to go? They are closely related questions. Ruling out software and programmed calculator solutions, there are standard vector plotting solutions to these questions. If you plan to take a USCG deck officer license exam then you will have to learn these proper vector solutions. The procedures are shown in Figure 1 primarily so you can test the approximations we give here. They are not complicated, but in practice there is rarely if ever any need for these formal solutions; the method we outline here that you can do in your head will meet most needs.

The problem with the formal vector solutions is you must know the set and drift of the current precisely or you get the wrong answer, and the only way to know the set and drift precisely is have a GPS. But if you have a GPS, you do not need the solutions in the first place.

First we concentrate on the set angle, since generally the direction we are going is much more important to safe navigation than how fast we are going. Second we make the assumption that the two questions have the same answer. Namely, if the current is setting us alpha (α) degrees to the right, then we correct for it by turning α degrees to the left. This is not strictly true mathematically, but it is close enough.

Next we divide all current directions up into 3 relative bearing categories: on the bow, on the beam, or on the quarter. To decide which case applies, draw in your desired course line from your present position to your destination as shown in Figure 2. Sketch a boat along that line pointed

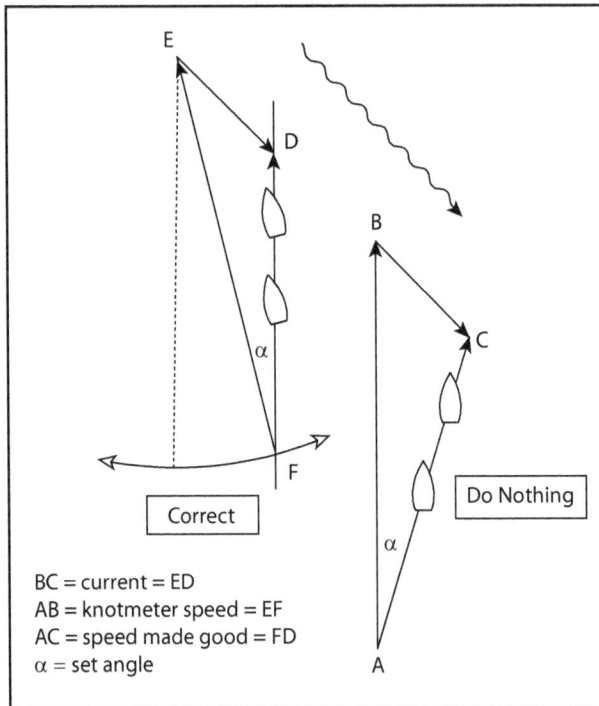

Figure 1. *Procedure for solving current vectors. We have shortcuts in the text; this is just the formal way for comparison.*

Do Nothing
is how you find out what will happed if you do not correct for the current.

(1) Draw a line AB in the direction you wish to proceed. Length AB = your knotmeter speed, ie at 6 kts make it 6 inches long or 6 cm long. Units do not matter as long as they are consistent.

(2) At B draw the current vector BC in the direction the current flows with length BC = current speed.

(3) Draw line AC, which is your SMG in direction CMG. The angle α is how much you will be set off your desired course as you proceed.

Think of this as the plot of an hour's run. You move from A to B, the water moves from B to C, so you end up moving from A to C.

Correct
is how you figure the course to steer to make good your desired course

(1) Draw a line FD of any length in the direction you wish to proceed.

(2) At any point D on this line, draw the current vector ED backward, into the direction the current flows from with length ED = current speed.

(3) At point E, swing an arc of length EF = your knotmeter speed. Mark the point F where it crosses the FD line. The angle α is how much you must turn into the current in order to track along your desired course. The length FD will be your SMG.

Again, in an hour's run, you move from F to E, steering into the current, and during this time the water moves from E to D, bringing you back to your desired track.

to the destination, and then draw in the current direction as it would intersect the boat in this orientation. Currents flowing toward you at 045 R ± 2 pts are "on the bow," 090 R ± 2 pts is "on the beam," and 135 R ± 2 pts is "on the quarter". Two compass points (2 pts) is 22.5°, but we are using this as shorthand only, so the decimals do not matter. The same definitions apply on the port side. For this reckoning we do not care what side of the boat the current is on.

Currents dead ahead (000 R ± 2 pts) or dead astern (180 R ± 2 pts) do not matter at all in this reckoning. These currents do not significantly change our direction, but just slow us down or speed us up by the speed (drift) of the current.

Our shortcut rule now is very simple. We developed this in the late 80's and it has withstood the test of time. We call α the set angle, meaning how much the current pushes us off our desired course—the difference between COG and the desired course. C is the current speed (its drift) and S is our knotmeter speed. Then

$$\alpha = C/S \times 60° \text{ for currents on the beam,}$$

and

$$\alpha = C/S \times 40° \text{ for currents on the bow or quarter.}$$

For example, for a current of 2 kts on the beam with a knotmeter speed of 6 kts, we will be set 2/6 x 60° = 20°, which we can easily figure on the wing. To correct for this, we would then turn 20° into the current and should track straight along our desired course.

The amount you get set for bow currents is the same as for quarter currents, since the lateral component of the current is the same. In this example it would be 2/6 x 40° = 40/3° = 13°. The only difference is how fast you will go. Your speed made good (SMG) going into the current (bow current) will be less than your knotmeter speed, and your SMG going down current (quarter current) will be more than your knotmeter speed.

With this approximation you can estimate your set and how to account for it as soon as you make some estimate of the current speed and direction. Sometimes you are not figuring the set to correct for it, but just accounting for it in your navigation.

Suppose you looked up the currents before a race and found they were expected to be 1 knot flowing parallel to the beach at this time. Now you are tacking up the beach at 5 kts into wind flowing along the beach, which puts the current roughly on your bow on both tacks. Therefore you are getting set by (1/5) x 40° = 8°. When you tack, your bow might turn through some 90°, but the angle between your port and starboard track lines will be more line 106°—each track is 8° more down wind than you would guess without this knowledge. Put another way, you have to over stand the mark by 8° to get there, with maybe a little in the bag for safety.

Quick algebraic estimates for the SMG are not as tidy, but these values are not often crucial to your navigation. Beam currents shift the knotmeter speed by about 6% of S at 20° set angle; about half that (3% of S) at 10° set; and about twice that (12% of S) at 30°, which is then getting close to the limit of this set angle approximation. In our example of a beam current of 2 kts on a knotmeter speed of 6 kts, we would estimate SMG of some 6 + 0.6 x 6 or 6.4 kts.

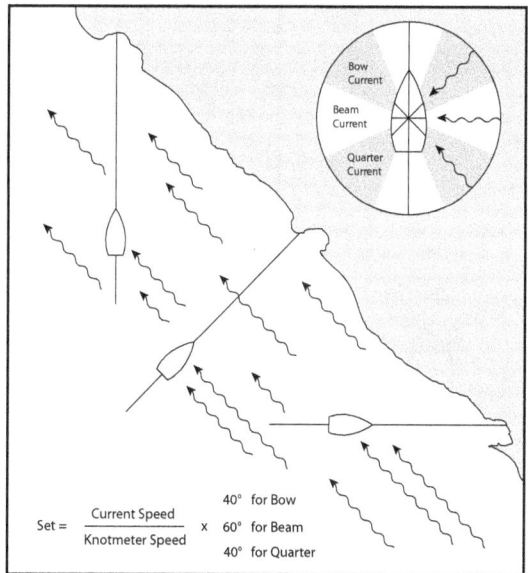

Figure 2. *Definition of relative current angles and an approximation for estimating set angle.*

For bow and quarter currents you can estimate the SMG as S ± 0.7 x current speed. This would be plus going downstream (quarter currents) and minus going upstream (bow currents). Going straight into the current or straight down current the SMG would be just S ± 1.0 x current speed.

The approximate answers are not right on as you can see in Figure 3, but they will almost always be well within the uncertainty of the current data. In other words, we never know the precise current speed and current direction at any moment, and if we did, they will likely change in 20 minutes or so. §

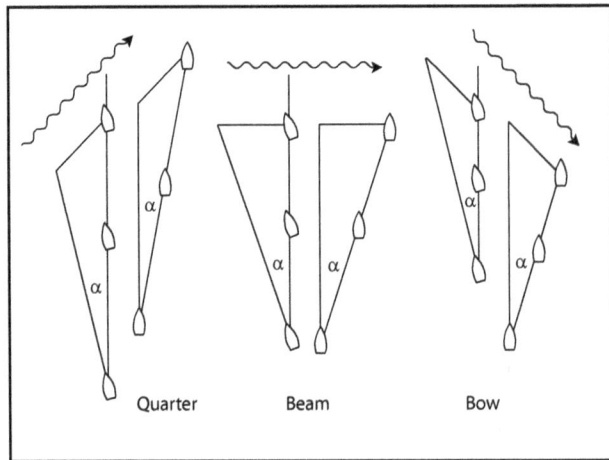

Current Corrections for Knotmeter Speed = 6.0, Current Speed = 2.0					
	Quarter		Beam		Bow	
	Correct	Do nothing	Correct	Do nothing	Correct	Do nothing
α	14° (13°)	11° (13°)	20° (20°)	18° (20°)	14° (13°)	17° (13°)
SMG	7.3 (7.4)	7.7 (7.4)	5.7 (5.6)	6.3 (6.4)	4.4 (4.6)	4.8 (4.6)

Figure 3. *Sample vector triangles for bow, beam, and quarter currents, along with the exact solutions and the approximates solutions in brackets.*

MORE CURRENT SAILING

In many inland waters tidal current flow is a dominating factor in navigation. In special cases like the Gulf Stream, it can also be crucial in the ocean. With a working GPS it is less of a challenge once underway because we can see directly from our recorded track through the water whether or not we are getting set off of our desired course line. If we are getting set off, we can steer into the current to get back onto our desired course line and then correct for the set to stay on this line. All of which assumes we have such options! Under sail we do not have this option going to weather, but sometimes do on other points of sail. In any event, what we will cover here can be useful even if we can't correct for it.

In principle the amount you correct is not the same as the amount you are getting set, but this is always a good starting point. If I am steering 300 and getting set to 320, then my first guess is to steer 280 to make good 300. But we always want to fine tune this to get it right. It could be that an average of 283 makes good 300, but by the time you learn that you are well off of your course line (waypoint to waypoint). So over correct to get back on the line, and then come back to 283. Good navigation means choosing the right waypoints in the first place then sail waypoint to waypoint, staying on your intended line. In the presence of underwater hazards this is absolutely crucial, but it is always good policy—otherwise you are not navigating, you are just out sailing.

Since we know we can't always correct for the current under sail, it often pays to think through the effect of the current before we leave. This prepares us for the magnitude of the effects we can't control, as well as making the adjustments more understandable when we can make them. Over the years we have developed several tricks and procedures at Starpath School of Navigation that make this job easier and more accurate.

One trick we call the Starpath 50-90 Rule, which can be used to predict current speeds in between slack and peak flow. A typical tidal current cycle goes from slack water to peak flow and back to slack water in some 4 to 7 hours, with the average being about 6 hours. Thus we divide the cycle from slack to peak into three time intervals, as shown in Fig 1. On a world average, the intervals would be about 1 hour each, but using thirds makes it more universal. Thus the rule is the current rises from slack to 50% of its peak in the first third, then to 90% in the second third, and finally to its peak in the last third. It is a way to approximate current speed at intermediate times for typical reversing tidal currents. The US Power Squadron has adopted this rule and offers work forms for applying it.

There are tables and diagrams in the NOAA Current Tables for figuring the intermediate speeds, but this rule is easier to remember and apply. Also strong currents in very constricted passes can rise and fall more quickly than this (called a hydraulic head). Such currents are usually noted in the current tables with a special intermediate speed table.

Once we have a way to estimate a current at any time, we can make the correction for it either properly with a vector plot as shown in Fig. 2 or you can use our trick for figuring it in your head shown in Fig 3. The estimate makes several math approximations, in addition to the basic assumption that the correction equals the amount you get set. In other words, this trick is telling us how much we get set if we do nothing, and we just assume we will go straight if we point into the current by the same amount. In practical navigation these estimates are plenty good enough because we do not know the currents well enough to justify a proper solution.

The third procedure to share here is our method of estimating the effective average current if you spend some time within a changing current pattern. In other words, what is the effective average current if you enter at one point in the cycle and leave at another? This important factor can be readily figured from the insert to Fig.1.

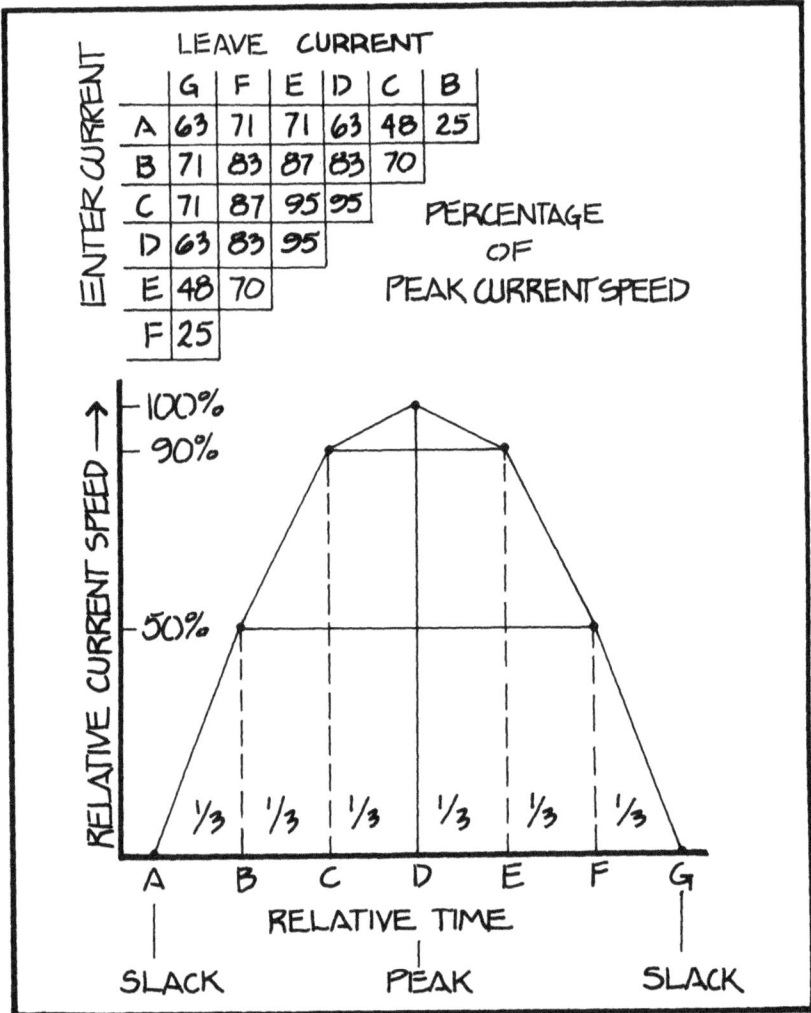

Figure 1. *A typical reversing current cycle, which on average would be 6 hr long, with each letter marking a 1-hr interval. If the peak current were 3.0 kts, then 50% is 1.5 kts, and 90% is 2.7 kts, at 1 and 2 hr into the cycle from slack.*

The inset shows the effective average current entering and leaving at specific points in the cycle. Entering at C and leaving at F would mean you will be set by an amount that is equivalent to a constant current of 0.87 x the peak current. Entering at A and leaving at D would be as if you were in a steady current of 0.63 x peak, which is the same as riding through the full cycle A to G. In our example, we enter at B and leave at D for an effective average factor of 0.83.

Not all, nor even most, cycles are symmetric like this, nor are they all 6 hours long, but this is the average, and the diagram can be used in halves for any time period using the third interval notation for the times. You can imagine two of these side by side, one flipped over for the other direction. The peak values and time scales are likely different for successive cycles.

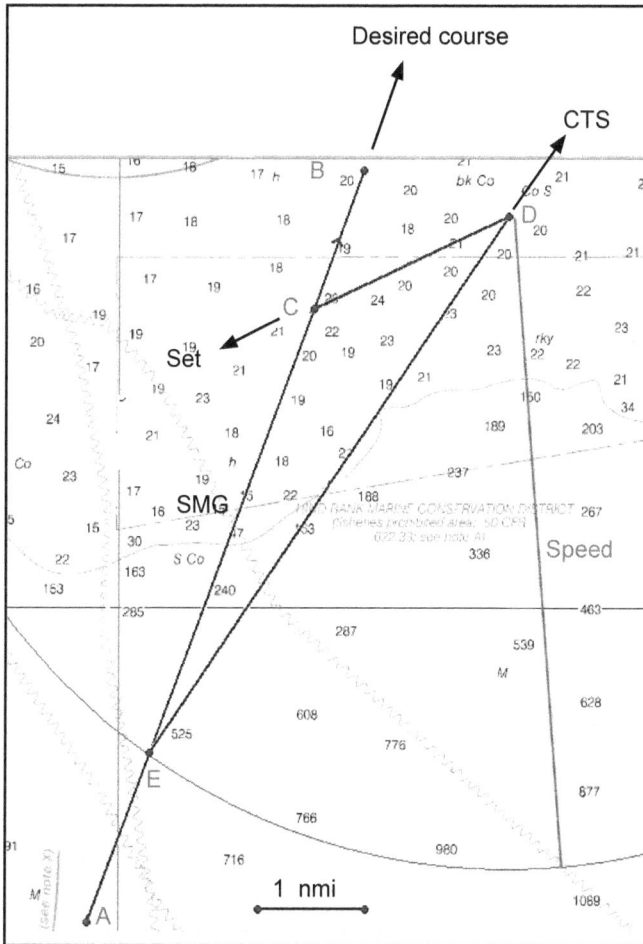

Figure 2. *Find Course to Steer (CTS) at a given Speed in the presence of current to make good a desired course.*

1. Draw line AB in the direction of your desired course

2. At any point C, extend your current vector back into the current, length = drift, direction = 180-set, with line CD

3. From point D, swing an arc of length = knotmeter speed so as to intersect AB at point E.

4. Then direction ED = CTS to make good your desired course, and EC will be your SMG.

In other words, in one hour you move from E to D and in that same hour the water moves from D to C, so you are actually progressing from E to C along your desired course but in this case (current forward of the beam) you will be making good a slower speed than your knotmeter speed.

This numerical example is for S=6, desired course = 020, set = 245 and drift = 2. The plotted solution here yields CTS = 033.6 and SMG = 4.4. The correction angle = 033.6 - 020.0 = 13.6°. If we use our trick formula, we get set = correction = (2/6)x40° = 13.3°, which only goes to show that it is not often we need to bring out these big guns!

As an example, consider a current crossing without GPS. Current tables tell us the current sets due west (flows toward 270 T); it is slack at 0900, and has a peak of 2.0 kts at 1200. Your destination is 5 nmi off in direction 045 T. Your knotmeter speed is 5.0 kts. You will be leaving at 10 AM. What correction would you make to your course to get there on a single heading?

A first estimate of the crossing time would be 1 hr, thus from Fig. 1 we enter the current at B and leave at C, which gives us a net average current of 0.70 x 2.0 = 1.4 kts. Our quick in the head estimate of the set would be (1.5/5) x 40, which we can figure at 1.5 x 8 = 10°, so this says we should sail 10° into the current (course 055 T) to get there on one heading. On this course we would first be over correcting, then later under correct-ing and end up on target. Not ideal since we wan-der off our track, but easy to figure on the wing. In waterways with hazards, we might want to break the trip up into smaller steps to stay closer to the intended track line. In any event, the diagrams provide the solution to any number of steps.

Plot this out more accurately with the method of Fig. 2 and you get the mathematically correct heading is 056.4° and the resulting speed made good (SMG) would be 3.91 kts. Our trick for fig-uring set angle does not give us SMG, but for cur-rents on the bow or beam, the SMG is less than knotmeter speed, and for quarter currents it is faster.

Figure 3 is another presentation of our ap-proximate solution, which is discussed in more detail in the previous article. §

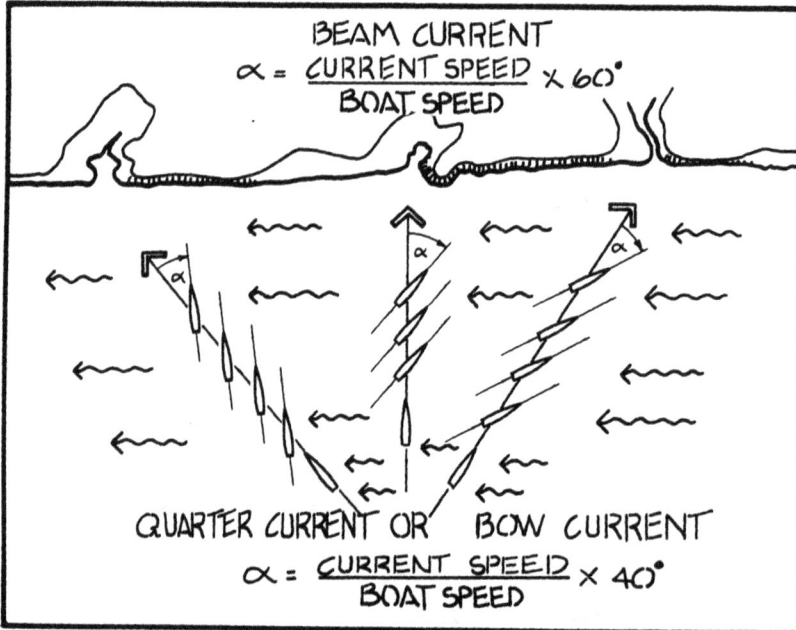

Figure 3. *Trick for estimating current set. Draw the desired course line across the current to decide if the current angle is closer to the bow, beam, or quarter. Bow and quarter corrections are the same, only the SMG changes. At a knotmeter speed of 6 kts crossing a 2-kt current on the beam, the set angle (α) is (2/6) x 60° = 20°. This same current on the bow or quarter would call for a correction of (2/6) x 40° = 13°.*

COASTAL CURRENTS

Current flow within a mile or two of a coastline is usually the result of a complex set of forces. Contributing factors include tidal current, wind-driven current, prevailing offshore ocean circulation, river runoff, water depth, and local currents running parallel and perpendicular to the shoreline caused by the surf. Unusual hydraulic currents also might flow along a coastline following long storms that piled up water against a turn in the coastline. These hydraulic currents can occur with no wind, no waves, nor any tidal changes, as the sea-surface slope readjusts to calm conditions. Near headlands, bays, or entrances to inland waters, the coastal flow also is strongly affected by the shape of the coastline.

Because so many forces influence the flow, it is difficult to predict coastal currents of interest to small-craft navigators without local knowledge. Nevertheless, these currents are important to navigation because they can severely hinder progress along routes exposed to sudden weather changes. The height and direction of swells also can change in a few hours with no change in local weather, as wave remnants of distant storms first reach the coast. Coastal currents can vary significantly in speed and direction at any one location and vary rapidly and irregularly from point to point along a coast. Although in many areas the currents farther offshore (off the continental shelf) are fairly well understood and documented in Sailing Directions, it is questionable whether much of this knowledge gained from extensive traffic of larger vessels farther offshore can be extrapolated shoreward into regions of soundings well onto the continental shelf (depths less than 100 fathoms).

Because there is so little data for the region that lies between the surf zone and the shelf, it is important to measure the current yourself as often as possible when traveling along close-in coastal routes. It might then be possible to correlate this information with the state of the tide,

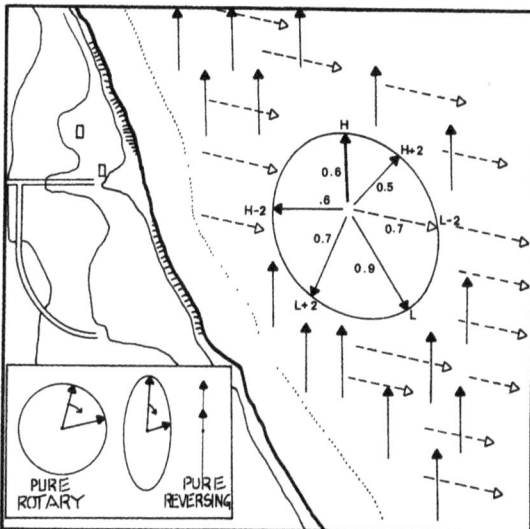

Figure 1. *Schematic rotating current diagram. As opposed to pure reversing currents found inland, which alternate their direction, coastal currents tend to rotate their direction with little or no change in speed. At the time of high water; this coastal region has a north current of 0.6 knot; at two hours before low water the current flows east-southeast at 0.7 knot. Note that the coastline shown could be 50 miles long or more. Arrows on these diagrams are usually scaled to the current speeds, but the location and overall size of the diagram has no significance. The current is not emanating from the location of the diagram on the chart, nor is the behavior it describes limited to that area. The diagram describes currents throughout that whole region of the coast. Also, the timing of the currents is not necessarily associated with the local tides. The tide stations used to reference the currents could be far from the current site. If the tide range at the reference station is notably different from the mean range, then the current speeds are likely more accurate if scaled according to the mean range.*

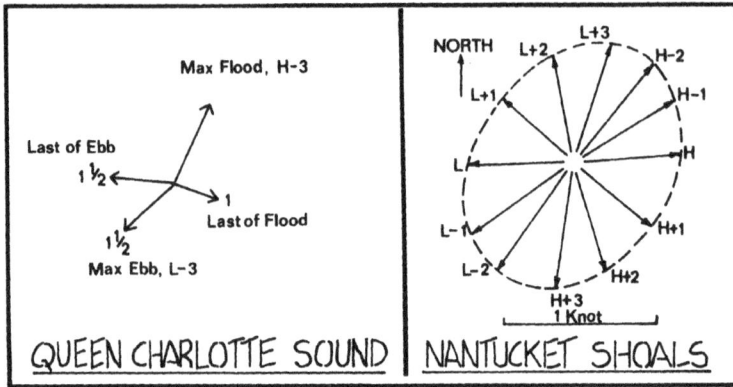

Figure 2. *Actual current diagrams for coastal waters of Queen Charlotte Sound, British Columbia (51° N, 129° W) from the Canadian Sailing Directions and from Nantucket Shoals, Massachusetts (41° N, 70° W), from the NOAA Current Tables. The styles of the two diagrams are different, but they convey similar information. The currents in Queen Charlotte Sound are much larger. In areas with mixed tides, the corresponding diagrams have two loops, reflecting the inequality of the highs and lows.*

wind speed and direction, lay of the land, and state of the surf, and gain some insight into the local current behavior that might help plan the rest of the trip. Nearshore current is a difficult subject in oceanography. When dealing with currents in these waters, your surprise threshold must be fairly high.

The tidal part of coastal current is typically rotary as opposed to the reversing currents found on inland waters (Fig 1). Pure rotary current changes directions without changing speed, so there are no slack waters. Current Tables, Sailing Directions, and some nautical charts provide diagrams that can be used to predict the speed and direction of rotating tidal currents based on the times of high and low tides at coastal reference stations. Examples are shown in Fig 2. Tidal currents in coastal waters rarely exceed 1 or 2 knots, and well away from the entrances to inland waters, the average values are much smaller—although as with all currents, coastal currents accelerate near headlands and diminish at the mouths of bays. There is also often enhanced and erratic current behavior near the continental shelf. For several reasons, a coastal route is usually better well onto or well off of the shelf, rather than following along its edge.

The tidal current rotations are also not purely circular near long open coastlines. The current direction does rotate (clockwise in the Northern Hemisphere) through 360° every 12 hours or so,

but the rate of rotation is not uniform and the speeds are not exactly the same in all directions. Most tidal streams well removed from inlets into inland waters flow faster and longer parallel to the coastline than perpendicular to it. Their rotation diagrams are not circles, but ellipses with the long axes lying parallel to the coastline. Near entrances to inland waters, on the other hand, the ellipses are more aligned with the inlet due to the flow in and out of the waterway.

In many areas, however, the rotary tidal flow is completely masked by wind-driven current whenever the wind blows steadily for half a day or longer. Expect this contribution to be approximately 3 percent of the wind strength, directed some 45° to the right of the wind direction in the Northern Hemisphere. Wind-driven currents tend to be stronger in heavy rains because brackish water slips more easily over the denser salt water below it. If Sailing Directions predict north-flowing currents of 1 or 2 knots, for example, expect the stronger end of the prediction when the wind blows toward the north and the weaker end of the prediction when the wind blows toward the south.

When waves strike the shore diagonally, they set up a current along the shore, inside the surf zone, flowing in the general direction of the wave motion. These currents inside the surf zone are not strong—0.5 knot might be typical for large waves—so these currents would rarely have direct influence on navigation. Nevertheless, water accumulated shoreward of the surf zone has to periodically escape seaward forming large rip current cells that can contribute to the prevailing flow outside of the surf.

Although nearshore coastal currents are difficult to predict with much dependability, every effort should still be made to establish the range of potential currents when planning coastal routes. Tidal Current Tables help in some locations, but Coast Pilots and Sailing Directions are the primary references in many areas. Whenever possible, also check with local fishermen who work both on and below the surface. In some areas, for example, commercial divers (who gather sea urchins, abalone, geoduck, kelp, herring roe, or sea cucumbers) are an excellent resource because they work daily in precisely the waters you might cruise, and they are aware of the current under many circumstances. Sport divers contacted through local diving shops also might be a source of local knowledge. Sailing or navigation schools that do regular tours in an area you might visit are naturally the best source when available.

There are ocean model predictions that might help in some waters. The best example I know of is presented in the Nanoos project (for waters off the coast of Oregon (Fig 3), which is a model prediction enhanced by coastal radar observations. Unfortunately, there are not many places with such good data. Output from the Global HYCOM model is available from several sources, some showing coastal waters (Fig. 4). The Navy has good data available to the public for Southern California, Gulf of Mexico, and Florida, and northward following the Gulf Stream, but that is then farther offshore. If you do find a model output online for

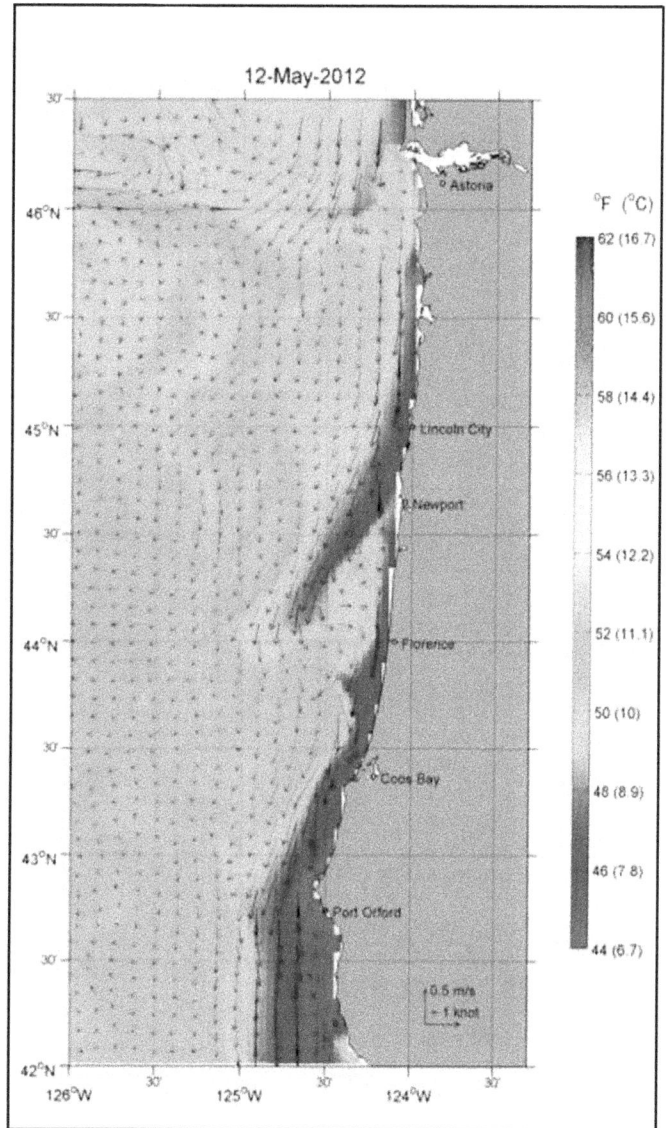

Figure 3. *A 48-hr coastal current forecast along the Oregon coast. This is perhaps the best data of this type available. See www. nanoos.org/nvs/nvs.php?section=NVS-Forecasts-OSU-ROMS.*

near coastal waters (there are several) then I would compare what they predict for the Oregon coast with the Nanoos data to help you evaluate their potential usefulness.

Another place to check model output would be any of the PORTS (Physical Oceanographic Real-Time System, tidesandcurrents.noaa.gov/ports.html) locations where there are buoys with current meters giving actual measurements.

Many mariners are already relying way too heavily on direct atmospheric model output for wind data ("GRIB weather maps"), without comparison with vetted maps and forecasts, but to do so with the ocean models is even a farther leap. We might argue that the GRIB wind forecast is better than none at all, but this might not be true with an unvetted model output for coastal currents! Ocean modeling not only depends on the accuracy of the atmospheric models, they also get (rough guess) less than 10% of the input data needed to pin the models down to known values.

In short, there is still a role for the navigator to use the best known data and principles to estimate the currents when no GPS is available, or to interpret and plan around what we learn from the GPS when we can measure the current effect on our progress. §

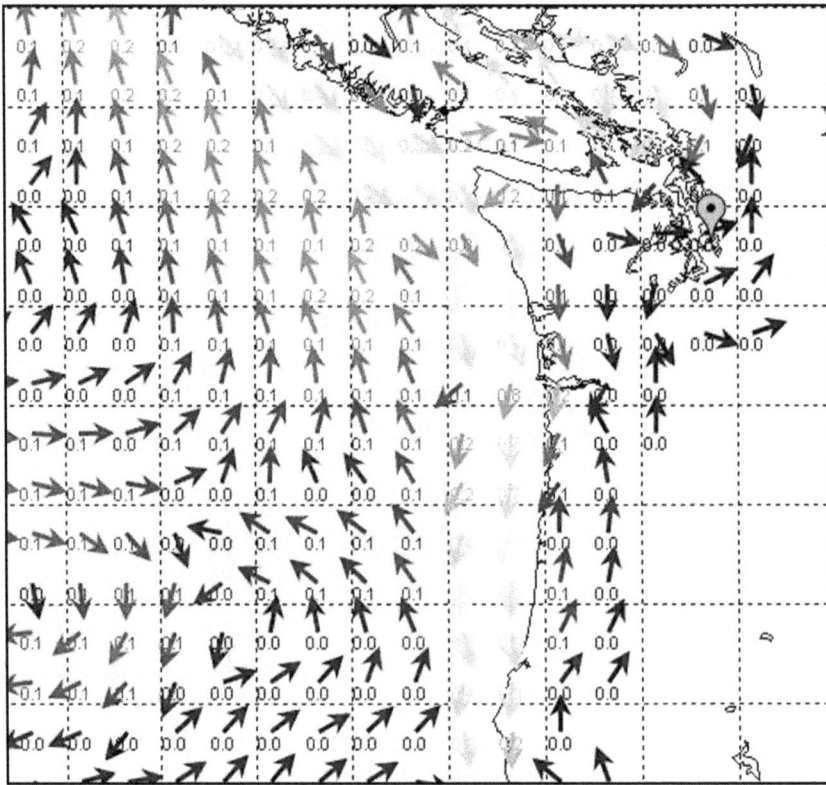

Figure 4. *HYCOM current predictions for the NW coast. These deep ocean model computations have some coastal affects included, but they are not dependable for nearshore coastal currents. The presentation shown here is from the commercial WeatherNet service from Ocens.com, which provides the predictions in GRIB format.*

OCEAN CURRENTS ARE NOT
WHAT THEY USED TO BE

O kay... This is not an article about climate change. Ocean currents are indeed what they used to be; it is just that we know now that they are not what we thought they were.

Bowditch teaches us in some detail the various ocean circulation patterns around the world (Figure 1). They have names, average speeds, directions, and water temperature. We have been taught to take these currents into account when planning ocean and coastal voyages––and they are the right answers to exam questions that come up in licensing and certification. We can learn the seasonal average values for specific locations from Pilot Charts (Figure 2). Boundaries of the Gulf Stream, called the North Wall and South Wall, are shown on the OPC map of 24-hr wind and waves.

While these ocean current data remain valid and helpful in many circumstances, we know now that they are a coarse outline of what the ocean surface flow really looks like at any one moment. We have learned very much more about the ocean in the past 5 years from international satellite measurements and from the development of numerical models of the ocean. Figure 3 shows a more realistic snapshot of the ocean surface. It is far more dynamic than we might have guessed from descriptions in early navigation and weather books. We have set up links to articles, videos, and other modern resources at www.starpath.com/currents. The latest *Bowditch* (2002) briefly mentions mesoscale eddies, but it predates new ocean research.

We are especially fortunate in most US coastal waters to have ready access to excellent real time coastal currents from HF radar measurements (Figure 4). These are the best real-time current data available. They also serve as a test for ocean model predictions. The BOM in Australia also

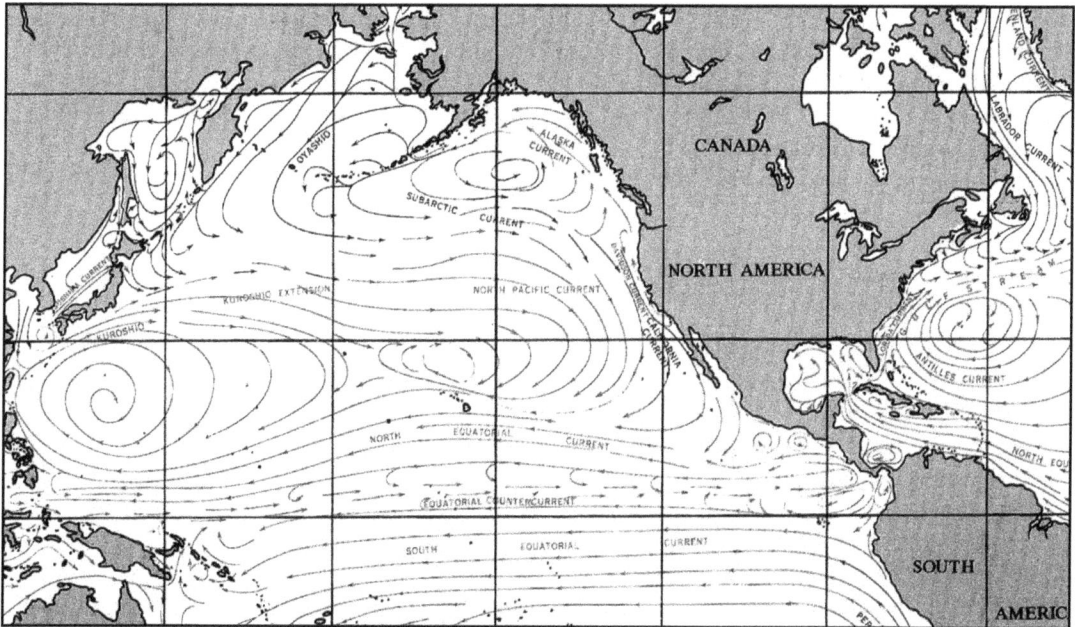

Figure 1. *Section of the Bowditch Stream Drift Chart, which remains one of the best overall outlines of ocean currents. See also the RSMAS site in the References.*

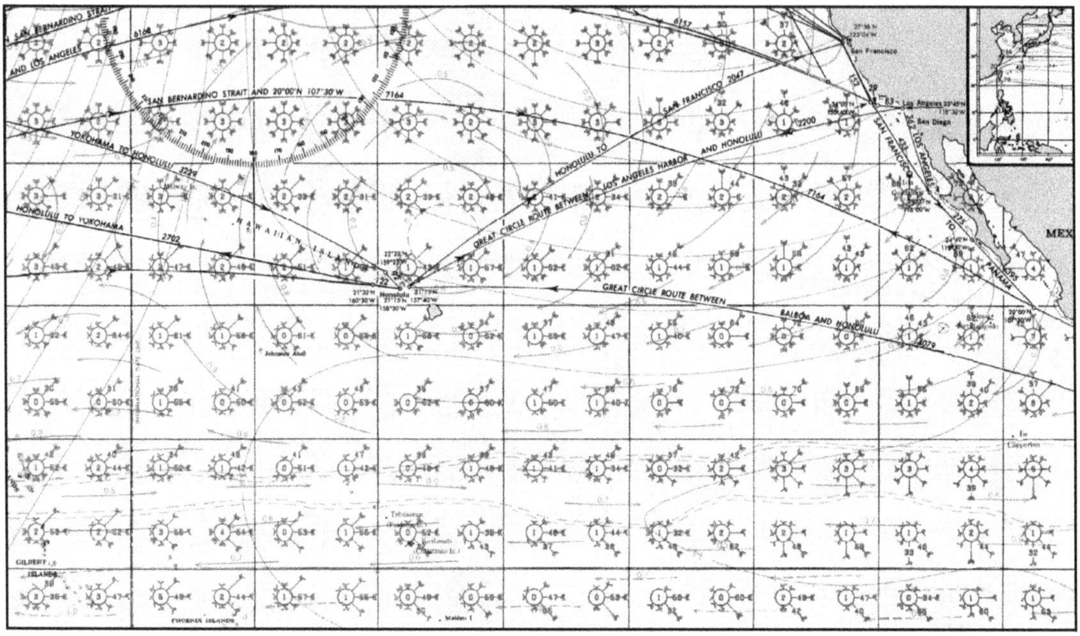

Figure 2. *Section of the May Pilot Chart, which remain the best quick source for climatic estimates of current flow. Green lines are currents with speeds in kts. Note the large gyre NE of Hawaii, consistent with the Bowditch prediction.*

coastal current predictions online, but they are small pictures, that require a subscription for more convenient format. Nevertheless, they do show that the common descriptions we used to use for these coastal currents are over simplified.

Once we leave the US coastal waters and travel outside the range of these HF Radar stations, we have more of a challenge in learning what others know about the currents we are sailing in. We have the Pilot Chats for the climatic averages, but for actual up to date data we must rely on numerical ocean prediction models. There are several versions operated by different agencies of the government.

There are several private companies that provide Gulf Stream predictions based on these models combined with annotated sea surface temperature measurements prepared by the Navy, and we can also track down much of that data online. Away from

the Gulf Stream and the Gulf of Mexico, we must turn to the model predictions.

The Gulf of Mexico is very well studied because the great Loop Current from the Gulf Stream makes the entire US East Coast vulnerable to oil spills in the Gulf. We had a close call with the Deepwater Horizon spill, but luckily the loop had pinched off into an eddy at the time (Figure

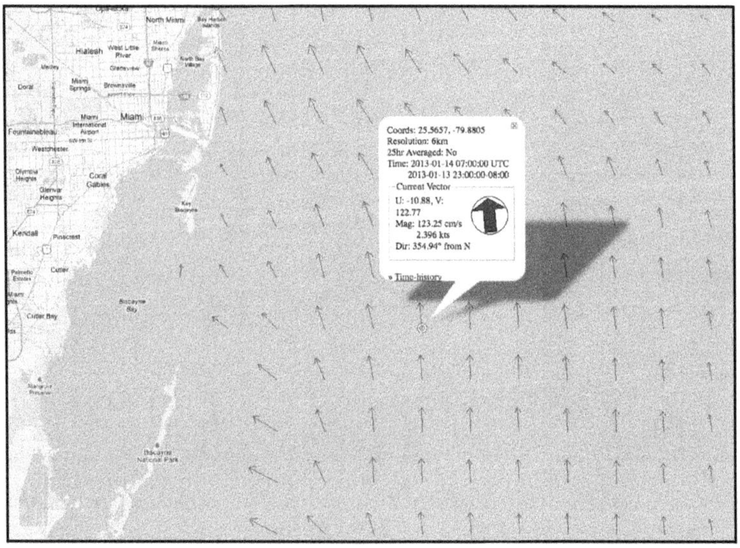

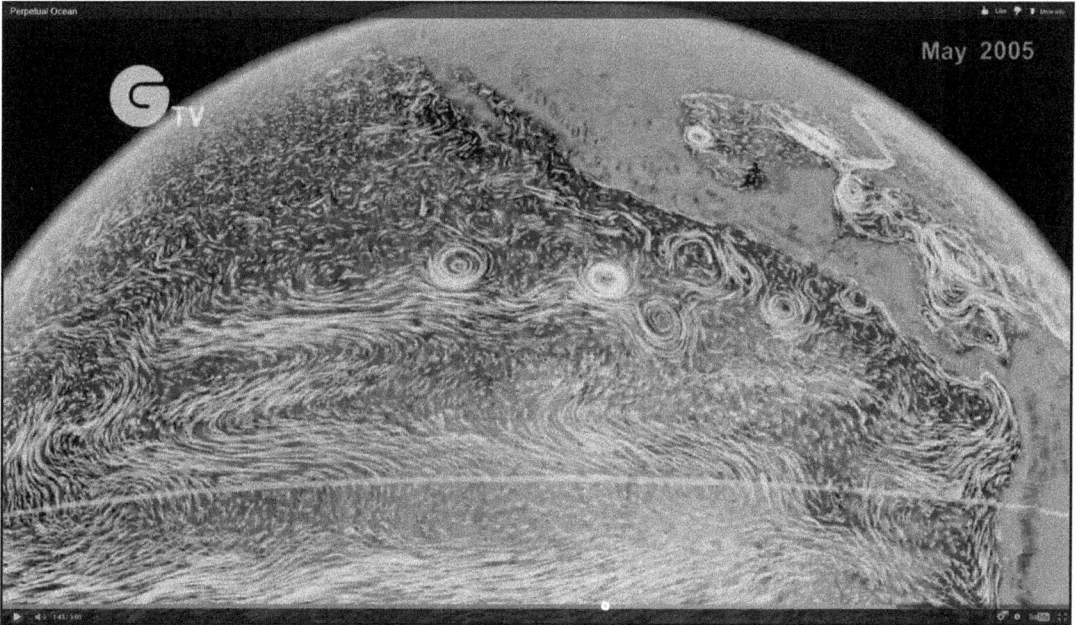

Figure 3. *A snapshot of May current circulation showing numerous eddies and meandering streams around the globe. These are model data, after assimilation of actual measurements. This is a screen capture from the excellent NASA video called Perpetual Ocean, www.nasa.gov/topics/earth/features/perpetual-ocean.html. It shows all oceans and seasons.*

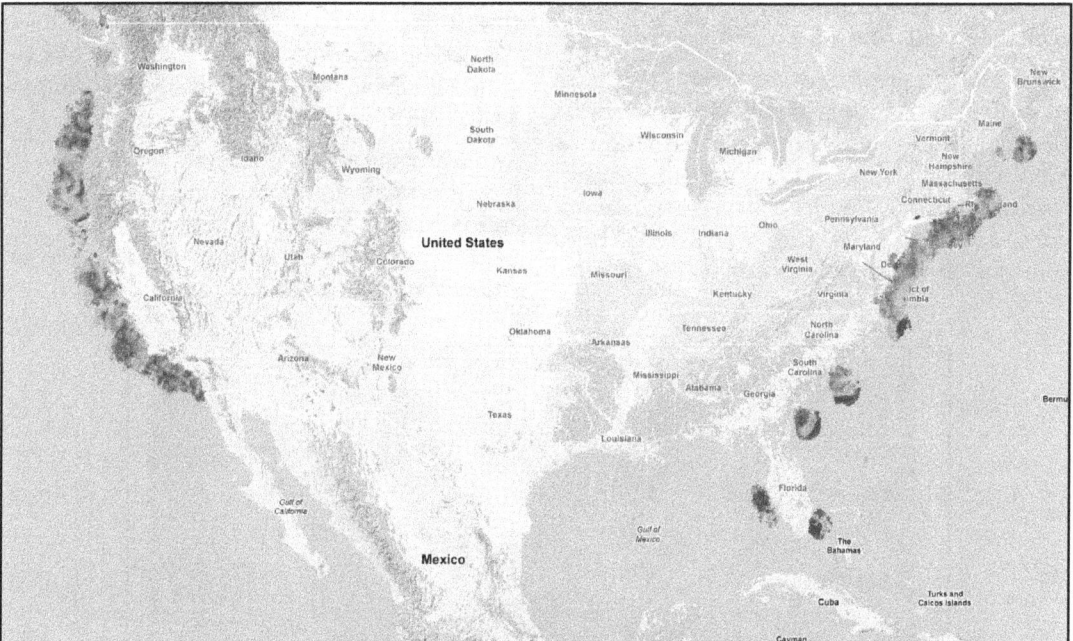

Figure 4. *Top. HF Radar stations with live coastal current data. Histories and averages are also available. If these data are available for your location then they will be your best source, and in some cases could be accessed via wireless connections underway. Facing page. HF radar current data from a Miami station, viewed from an online Internet link. They also have links showing recent and long term history of the current values at any location in the data field.*

5). Ocean currents would have been a lot more in the news than they are now had that not been the case.

Recently the Ocean Prediction Center (OPC) added links to the RTOFS (Real Time Ocean Forecast System) model data, but these are more schematic pictures than real numerical data we can navigate with. We can at least see that things are very dynamic. The model is based on the HYCOM model (www.hycom.org). Better detail can be seen in the US Navy presentation listed in the References.

The easiest to use online source of Navy data is from their NCOM model, a sample of which is shown in Figure 6. As far as I know, at the moment the only way to get this data at sea without an Internet connection is have someone get it online for you and email it to you, which is not at all unheard of with the convenience of satellite phone or SSB connections.

We do have direct access underway to three other ocean models in GRIB format that can be requested by email and then displayed underway. Two are public services created by individual mariners (Jim Corenman via saildocs.com and Eric Baicy, via svsarana.com); the third is a commercial service from ocens.com.

The RTOFS predictions can be obtained at sea from the latest version of the SailDocs ViewFax program. The data are requested by lat-lon region, and available every 12 hours, with 5 days of forecast.. The OSCAR model data from svsarana. com is a sliding 5-day average analysis, without forecasts. Ocens.com is presently offering the

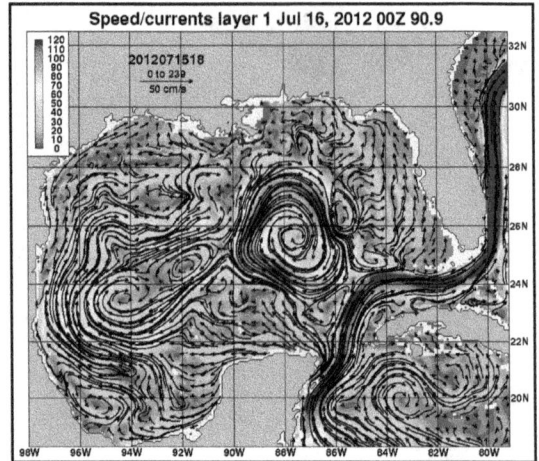

Figure 5. *US Navy HYCOM data at the time of the oil spill. This eddy in the Gulf shows up more often as just the end of a large loop in the Gulf Stream that penetrates in the Gulf.*

Global HYCOM data, but their system is flexible and they can change sources or add new ones.

Samples are shown in Figure 6, which when compared with each other and with the NCOM model for the same time and place shows a very important point about the model analysis—they do not agree with each other! This is just one comparison. Mariners will have to make their own study and compare with what they observe to decide which model might help with their navigation needs.

Clearly the flow is not as simple as we would have guessed from our early training, all models agree with that, but it is not clear which model offers mariners the best guide. As we learn more we will post it at www.starpath.com/currents.

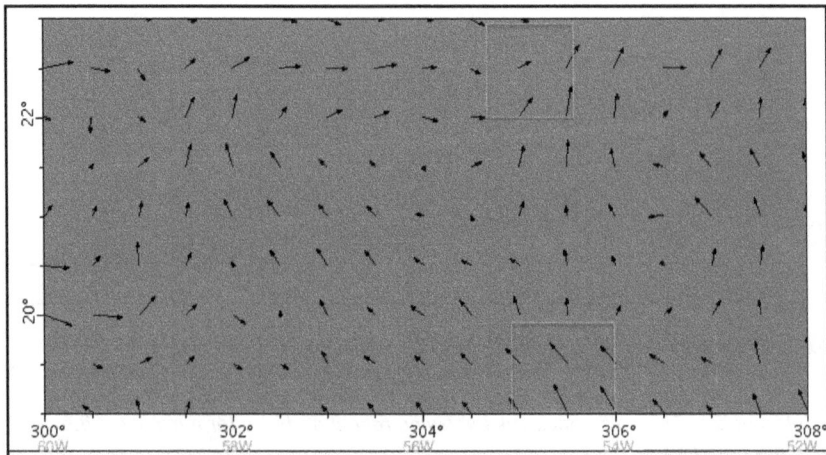

Figure 6. *Tropical Atlantic current predictions from several ocean models valid on Mar 23, 2013. The models are explained in the References. The two red boxes mark two 1°x1° regions for comparison. Bottom Facing page is the Navy NCOM model, available online but not underway. Speeds in the boxes vary from 0.2 to 0.4 kt. Top is the OSCAR data from svsarana. Speeds in the boxes vary from 1 to 2 kts. Middle is the RTOFS data from ViewFax; speeds in the boxes vary from 2 to over 4 kts. Bottom is the Global HYCOM from Ocens. Boxed speeds vary from 1 to 2.5 kts. There is some element of pattern matching in the full regions shown, but almost conspicuous disagreement at specific locations.*

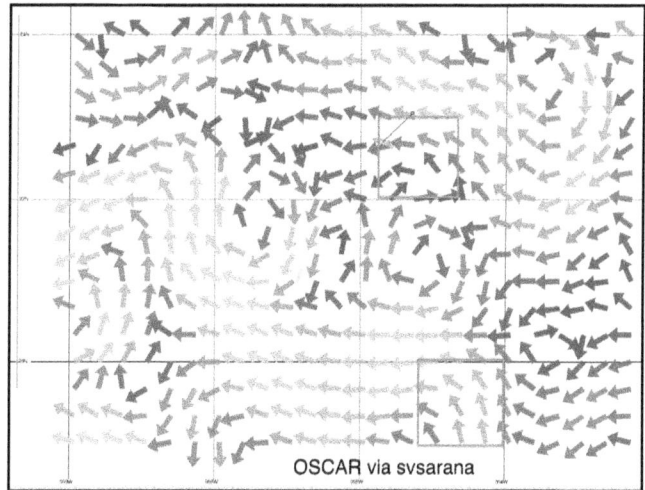

OSCAR via svsarana

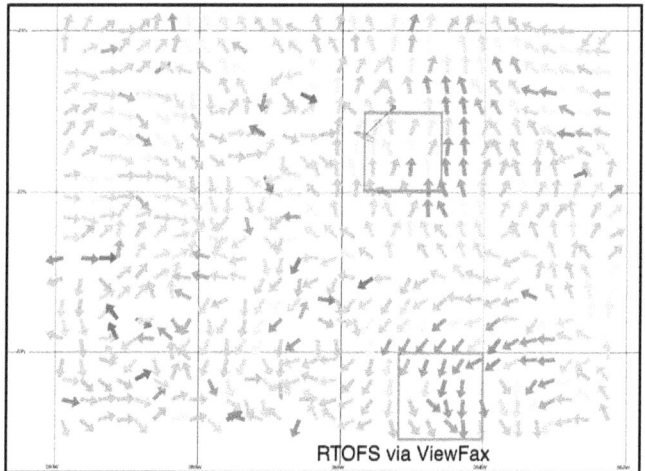

RTOFS via ViewFax

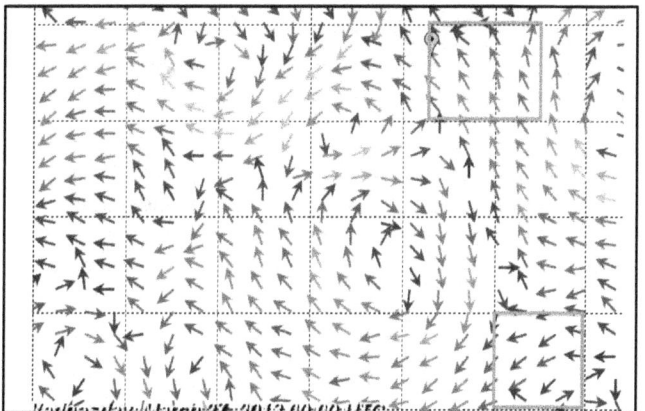

Post script

It is tempting to go back to the title and say, "Well... Maybe the currents are what they used to be, and the models are just all wrong!" Clearly some are wrong.

But that is not productive. Global current flow is more complex than was known 10 years ago, and these models do predict the behavior of the strong boundary currents (Gulf Stream, etc) very well and more to the point they do a pretty good job in the meander and eddy formation along the edges of the boundary currents, and in the prominent source regions of msesoscale eddy production.

Sailors in slow boats crossing oceans (let alone ocean rowers) simply present a challenge the models are not yet set up to solving. We want the set and drift every where, as accurately as possible. Half a knot does not mean much to a ship traveling 20 kts, but it can be crucial to a sailboat in light air. On the other hand, if we find a 2-kt eddy, we are off like a rocket.

We need to start comparing predictions with what we can measure from the boat, and eventually we will home in on the best data. The models are all evolving as well. It is a work in progress.

Recently in the preparation of new training materials in celestial navigation, we analyzed a couple ocean passages I did back when we had only celestial navigation to go by. These passages call for careful dead reckoning (DR). Almost always the DR made good sense compared to the position fixes done every day or two. But once in a while, the DR would be way off by 30 miles or more in one day. Then it would be good again, even though the procedures were not changed.

After studying ocean currents now for some time, I suspect these anomalies (which could not be accounted for by blunders) might be traced to transient mesoscale eddies that just took the boat off track as we crossed them. Without electronics, there would be no way to detect that. §

References for Ocean Currents*	
Sources and tactics	*Modern Marine Weather, 2nd Ed.* by David Burch
Excellent general resource	oceancurrents.rsmas.miami.edu
Ocean Prediction Center	www.opc.ncep.noaa.gov
Pilot Charts, Bowditch, etc	www.starpath.com/navpubs
HF Radar Currents	cordc.ucsd.edu/projects/mapping/maps
RTOFS	polar.ncep.noaa.gov/ofs/viewer.shtml?-natl-cur-0-large-rundate=latest
RTOFS in GRIB format	www.siriuscyber.net/wxfax
OSCAR	www.oscar.noaa.gov
OSCAR in GRIB format	www.svsarana.com/oscar
HYCOM	www7320.nrlssc.navy.mil/GLBhycom1-12/skill.html
HYCOM in GRIB format	www.ocens.com
US Navy NCOM	ecowatch.ncddc.noaa.gov/erddap/griddap/NCOM_sfc8_agg.html
AVISO general reference and data	www.aviso.oceanobs.com/en/applications/ocean/mesoscale-circulation.html
* Links, news, and resources kept up to date at www.starpath.com/currents	

INDEX

Symbols
4-5-6 Rule, 80
34-kt Rule, 85–88

A
Annotated Navigation Rules, 9
ASCAT, 81–84
Automatic Identification System (AIS), 6, 20

B
barometer, 14–15, 55, 77–80
bow angle, 2–3

C
celestial navigation, 3, 12, 17–18, 38, 57, 64–67,
    72–75
chart. *See* nautical chart, echart, weather map
Chart No. 1, 5, 21, 29–31
Chart table, 52–56
Climatology of Global Ocean Winds (COGOW),
    83
Coast Pilot, 5, 30–31, 62, 107
Code of Federal Regulations (CFR), 15–16, 31,
    71
COG and SOG, 3–4, 14, 27–28, 33, 55, 97, 99
COLREGS, 7–9, 61
communication, 2–3, 23, 26, 45, 68–71
compass use, 2, 17–18, 28, 32–34, 38–42,
    54–55, 57, 59
corner effect, 93–95
Cosco Busan, 6, 21, 37
course box, 2, 4, 54, 55
currents
    eddies, 109–111
    Gulf Stream, 14, 101, 107, 109–110, 112
    HF Radar, 109–112, 114
    HYCOM, 107–108, 112, 114
    in ECS, 25
    NCOM, 112–114
    OSCAR, 112–114
    rotary, 106
    RTOFS, 112
    Starpath 50-90 Rule, 101
    wind-driven, 32–34, 105–106

D
dead reckoning (DR), 14, 32–35, 57–60, 114

E
echart, 23–28, 37
Electronic Bearing Line (EBL), 2–4, 47
Electronic Charting Systems (ECS), 4, 19–21,
    23–28, 97
Exxon Valdez, 6

F
Facebook, 95
fog, 44–50, 89–92

G
Google Earth, 19–20
GPS, 3, 5–6, 14, 36–37
    jamming, 36
GPX, 20–21
Gulf Stream. *See* currents

I
International Code of Signals (ICOS), 68–71
iPhone, 9, 20, 24, 69, 70–71, 72

K
Kamal, 38

L
leeway, 25, 28, 32–35, 59–60
local knowledge, 5, 57, 105–107
local time, 10–12, 15, 31
logbook, 2, 4, 13–16, 55

M
Mariner's 1-2-3 Rule, 85–88
Marine Weather Service Charts, 13, 29
Memory-Map Navigator, 24
Modern Marine Weather, 13, 84, 85, 114

N
National Hurricane Center (NHC), 85–88
Nautical Almanac, 12, 64–66
nautical chart, 29–31, 40–42, 53. *See also* Chart
    No. 1
navigation
    electronic. *See* electronic charting systems,
    radar, AIS
    history, 36, 73–75
    procedures, 26–28
    to weather, 32–35

Navigation Rules, 7–9, 45, 50
nav station, 52–56
nist.gov, 10–12
NMEA, 3

O

Ocean Prediction Center (OPC), 92, 109–110, 114
OpenCPN, 19–21

P

Pilot Charts, 20, 24, 59, 83, 109–110, 114
plotting tools, 43, 56

Q

QuikSCAT, 36, 82–83

R

racing tactics, 4, 15, 33–35
radar, 2–4, 14, 23, 26, 28, 39, 41–42, 44–50, 82, 107
relative bearings, 2–3, 97

S

S-57 (ENC format), 19–21, 21
SailDocs, 112–114
sextant, 2, 28, 55, 66, 69, 72–75
    Davis Mark 3, 38
    piloting, 36–43
ship reports, 15, 79
sight reduction tables, 64–67

Somali pirates, 5
Superstorm Sandy, 87
Swinomish Slough, 7

T

taffrail log, 5
three-arm protractor, 40
Timekeeping, 10–12

U

units, 2, 29
USCG, 7–9, 11–12, 16, 36, 61–62, 72, 85, 97
US Navy, 14, 65, 107, 112, 114
UTC, 10–12, 66, 82–83, 87

V

vector solutions, 26
VHF, 8, 13, 29
VMG, 4

W

WAAS, 33, 36–37, 39
waypoints, 4, 14, 26–28, 62, 97, 101
weather maps, 10, 12, 15, 20, 24, 70, 78, 80, 107

X

XTide, 19

Z

Zone Time, 11–12
zulu, 11–12

www.ingramcontent.com/pod-product-compliance
Lightning Source LLC
Chambersburg PA
CBHW080518110426
42742CB00017B/3156